UNSTOPPABLE: PASSION UNLEASHED

Once It Starts, Who Can Stop It?

CRYSTAL SCOTT, LMFT, M.A., B.S.

authorHOUSE®

AuthorHouse™
1663 Liberty Drive
Bloomington, IN 47403
www.authorhouse.com
Phone: 1 (800) 839-8640

Published by AuthorHouse   10/11/2019

ISBN: 978-1-7283-3053-2 (sc)
ISBN: 978-1-7283-3052-5 (e)

Print information available on the last page.

Any people depicted in stock imagery provided by Getty Images are models,
and such images are being used for illustrative purposes only.
Certain stock imagery © Getty Images.

This book is printed on acid-free paper.

CONTENTS

FOREWORD

I met Crystal at a book fair and it was clear to me that she was gifted. How do you have a gift of igniting passion in people? Well, read on and find out. Crystal will not only open your eyes to the passion inside of you; but she will also make sure you see it so clearly; you can't deny why it's there. Humbly, I am grateful for our meeting; it wasn't by chance. Crystal's message to you is on time!

In this book, you will learn how your ignited passion is not only for you; but also to help others. If you are ready to be thrilled, challenged, confronted with truth, and see the light inside you and others; this is the book to help you while on your journey. Passion is inside and outside of you. So, don't try to control it. Unleash it!

Candace Smith

INTRODUCTION

I met Candace at the Tulisoma book event in Dallas TX, August, 2019. She was like a breath of fresh air as she spoke with me about passion. Our spirits connected as we engaged in discourse. Candace spoke into my current life and she touched on points I have been pondering for a while. Confirmation through our conversation ignited and reawakened thoughts and passions in me. I could hardly sit in my seat. As time went on throughout the day, I realized what my next book would be about.

Motivation to write about passion is also greatly influenced by the many times I have spoken with patients who have asked: "How do I find out what my passion is?" My initial response is this: passion is not limited to one thing or one area. Then I describe a definition of passion. According to Dr. Robert Vallerand, Professor of Psychology in Canada: "Passion is a strong inclination towards a self-defining activity (object, person, or belief) that people love, that they consider important, and in which they devote significant amounts of time and energy." Then I have patients to consider what they would do with the same commitment and fervor, that they currently do for a paycheck and benefits; it is something they would do for free if they were financially well off and did not need to earn an income.

Taking patients through this exercise tends to lead to responses ranging from identification of a few examples, to arriving at a complete blank. When a blank is experienced I encourage individuals and ensure it is never too late to become aware of what touches you passionately. I then explore with patients and provide psychoeducation as to why some people are challenged in the area of connecting with passion, as well as help with understanding ways to overcome challenges and barriers to passion awareness.

Some good examples that describe the meaning of passion and distinguishes between a hobby or pastime is a person who plays a piano versus a pianist; a person who tells jokes versus a comedian; and a person who regularly sings in the shower versus a music artist. Through principles of self-awareness, I encourage individuals to consider how passion is unveiled. Self-awareness is necessary in order to know and understand yourself and get in touch with passion. Consequently, when there are many people shaping your beliefs and influencing your life, this can create difficulty finding your own voice and becoming aligned with who you are to the point that you realize your passion.

In this reading you will learn many aspects of passion. I know you must have heard passion discussed in a very general sense; however, there is a psychology to all this "passion" stuff that not very many people consider. In fact, although you will deal with passion in this material as related to your own personal growth and development; you will come to know (and might be surprised) about the many, many other variables involved in effectively understanding passion. Sure, the concept of passion is sometimes tossed around in discussion casually and often times not considered for its full value. However, I have delved deeply into this topic in a way that I know you will enjoy.

Each Chapter of this book builds on the previous, providing you with information to help you think differently about passion, to the end that you will operate in your true passions effectively from this point on. *Chapter I* is passion described. The etymology of passion has its roots in the Latin word *passio*. *Passio* means to suffer. By virtue of the fact that you are passionate means you intensely love and value; therefore, you will experience discomfort while living a passionate life.

You will experience discomfort when people do not respect your passion. You will experience discomfort when you are up against opposition as related to your passion. You will also experience discomfort when you become weary along the way; but passion won't allow you to quit, it drives you. Keep the definition and understanding of passion in mind as you continue on in this reading and everything will come together and form an aha! moment for you.

Chapter II deals with doubt. Be certain, doing what you are passionate about does not mean you will not experience doubt, doubt will creep in. I am confident that information provided in this chapter will resonate with thoughts and concerns you have about passion, and will increase clarity regarding roadblocks that adversely impact passion in your life. You will learn how to foster a mindset of tenacity that overshadows moments of doubt. Chapter *III* focuses on overcoming challenges and provides insight regarding strategies you will need to get through tough times and follow through with your passion. Discovery of suitable tools for overcoming challenges to passion is delineated in this chapter, including effective decision-making and keys for living a balanced life.

In *Chapter IV,* I have provided examples of what passion unstopped looks like, by spotlighting characters who demonstrate a profound illustration of passion against all odds. As you allow yourself to be enveloped by these accounts, pay close attention to how you respond. In doing so, you might gain greater awareness about your passion. *Chapter V* contains personal accounts of my life as I have encountered times of passions. For sure, in my fifty plus years of living, I have experienced upheavals, as well as successes related to passion. I am confident that you will gain a sense of encouragement to valiantly continue on in your pursuit of a passion-filled life. You are encouraged to cultivate a mindset to pay it forward in *Chapter VI.*

Once you have a grounded understanding of how to recognize what you are passionate about, make paying it forward your commitment. When you are able to competently and confidently move forward, living a satisfying life filled with passion, share your story with others. Others need what you have gained and you will be proud for paying it forward. Finally, Chapter *VII* contains surveys and a life satisfaction questionnaire to help you with increased self-awareness and get you closer to understanding and unleashing passion. The more you know; the more you will become motivated to engage your passion. In fact, your passion will not be ignored. Once it starts, who can STOP it?

"There is no passion to be found playing small—in settling for a life that is less than the one you are capable of living."

Nelson Mandela

CHAPTER I

PASSION DESCRIBED

Her name is passion. There are times when she appears awkward and uncertain, but is she really? Or has she been colored and conditioned by her circumstances? Passion is just being careful; you see, she has been judged and talked about because she is so different from those who are around her. If you do not know her, you might think she is timid and aloof. It might be difficult to get into her space at times because she is usually very focused and intentional about her moves; and being distracted and disrupted is one of her peeves. But once you get to know her; she is fiery, quite intense, and loads of fun to be around. One moment you might notice her calm and relaxed, and the next moment she is vigorously engaging when she is stirred.

Passion has been misunderstood many times; therefore, she is sometimes apprehensive about who she shares her thoughts and emotions with. She has also been criticized for being too excitable and has been labeled as "doing too much." But passion does what passion is. She is a fire that cannot be doused.

Throughout her maturation, passion has thought about many things she could do and how she would impact the world. She knew that she embodied greatness; but when she started out, she was not in a supportive environment. Passion had to fight her way through negativity and even her own self-doubt. Self-defeating thoughts would creep in every now and then when she would reflect on how she becomes so excited about all of her possibilities. Then others would come along and throw shade. They would zap the energy right out of passion; but passion would never completely go away.

Sure, there are people who love to hang around her and benefit from her high times of excitement. These are the people who are also energy vampires. The moment passion is raring and, on a roll; she is cut down by someone who reminds her of times she has started out and not followed through. Regardless, passion prevails. She separates to reset because she must. Passion is fully aware of what she needs in order to keep herself from losing sight of what is important. Also, she remembers what happened one time when she was really down in the dumps and lost touch with herself for a period in her life.

Passion was working hard and doing her thing, but she had no balance to her life. She was on 24/7. She was so caught up in who she is organically, she did not realize what was happening to her. Passion burned herself out and then she began to wonder if she was losing the essence of herself. Of course, the naysayers and doubters would come along and discourage her, to keep her at a level that they could deal with her. Why? Because when passion is in her element, she is unstoppable and can be intimidating.

The moment passion experienced burnout she went on what seemed like a sabbatical. She went from being upbeat and on all the time, to extreme mediocrity and an average existence. Passion began hanging around people who were happy with doing the bare minimum. In fact, it seemed as if she was a little relieved to have a moment to take a break, to get away from herself. She thought, maybe the others are right; maybe I am doing too much. Am I really who I say and think I am? So, she continued with a sort of lackadaisical kind of life. Some around her were happy to have passion down to their level. Others whispered behind her back and said: "I knew it was all a show, she couldn't keep up the façade for long. There were some who were bold enough to stand face-to-face with passion and call her a fraud, a fake, and a phony.

One day passion was alone at home and she wondered how did she get so far down. She wondered how did her life go so far to the left that she did not recognize herself. She sat and reflected, and realized how she got off track. While she was trying to add a little balance to her life she got caught up in mediocrity, but she was not happy. When passion is not doing what passion is designed to do, what was once upbeat and energetic becomes depressed and sad.

Passion did a good job of helping others feel comfortable because she put her fire out to fit in with those who never really understood and respected the essence of who she is. She gained the favor of her average companions, but she lost her since of self and purpose. Passion had a decision to make. She knew she would never be truly happy until she decided to get back in touch with who she is naturally. She also realized that ignoring who she is will not simply make her traits go away. Passion unattended leads to a boring, depressed, lackluster state that cannot be denied.

What passion does from this point on makes the difference, turns the tide, and sets her back on course. She now has a point of reference for dealing with challenging times, times when faced with either getting off track or staying the course. What does passion do? Passion disciplines and balances herself to remain centered and focused on her essence. She looks at herself in the mirror and there the sparks begin again. She sees what she was missing during the time she took her eyes off of herself. From this point forward, passion vows to never discount or diminish herself to please others, and thus; her journey continues.

Two Types of Passions

I introduced to you Dr. Robert Vallerand, Psychology Professor in Canada, at the very beginning of this reading. Dr. Vallerand's work is proficient in supporting my position on passion. Therefore, I engage his research to expand your knowledge of two types of passion, in the following summary: According to the Dualistic Model of Passion (DMP) there is *harmonious passion and obsessive passion.* Harmonious passion means to be well-proportioned, compatible, and with a sense of peace that accompanies; and there is no conflict. Obsessive passion is identified as all-consuming, tormenting, neurotic, inescapable, and pathological in nature.

Although I will discuss, more in depth, these two differing characteristics of passions; this does not mean you will only be either harmoniously passionate or obsessively passionate. There might be areas of your life that drive you passionately in a harmonious way and others that drive you obsessively. What matters is how you are attached to the thing, activity, or person in a passionate manner. Understanding your motivation for your passion can help you to make good, healthy decisions about how you direct your energy and time.

Harmonious Passion. The best way to help you understand harmonious passion is to have you consider passion that results from a sense of self-government, and the ability to be independent and self-determined. What is important to note here is that harmonious passion also shares some of the same qualities as *intrinsic motivation.* Vallerand posits: the difference is that intrinsic motivation lacks the internalization in one's identity, that is experienced with harmonious passion.

As I think about the autonomous perspective associated with harmonious passion, I recall the stages of human development. The second stage of human development is age 2-3 years old. Theorist Erik Erikson suggests that this stage is the stage of autonomy versus shame and doubt. In this example, it makes sense why some people experience a difficult time with harmonious passion. Pay careful attention here. Parenting and education play a critical role during this age. When interaction and develop goes well, the child is well-adjusted psychologically. The child is more likely to engage her will. She learns by what is imitated or modeled, language develops properly, she learns how to demonstrate self-control, engage in appropriate fantasy play, and is less likely to develop a core pathology of compulsive behavior. (*See illustration 1*).

Ages 2-3
Psychosocial Crisis: Autonomy
versus shame and doubt
Ego Quality: Will
Central Process: Imitation
Developmental Task:
Language development, self-
control, fantasy play
Core Pathology: Compulsion

(Stage of development Illustration 1)

Conversely, the child's ability to adjust well psychologically might become compromised if parenting and education does not represent healthy interaction that fosters adaptability. When a child is in this stage of development, some parents are not skilled at honing what might be a harmonious passion for the child. Parents and pre-school teachers focus on getting the child to behave appropriately and conform to expectations. Of course, the child needs guidance and requires training and discipline. But it is needful for those overseeing such processes to possess adequate knowledge and training of what is healthy, of what the child uniquely needs, and of approaches that best suit the child specifically. This way the child could develop a healthy ego, autonomy, and a determined will. If not, the child experiences shame and doubt; and successive stages of development could prove challenging.

Now let's tie these understandings together. We observe a child between 2 and 3 years of age. The child is attempting to demonstrate autonomy, or self-government. The child wants to pour her own cup of milk. The parent knows the child cannot pour the milk. The child sees no limits until the parent says, you can't hold the jug; you are not big enough. This is a critical time during development when a child either believes she can, or begins to doubt she can.

Although she might not have the language to articulate what this experience is like, if the child continues to experience such interactions throughout development: experiences of being told she is not big enough, or old enough, or skilled enough; these interactions shape her sense of self and autonomy. Do

I think people intend to hurt and limit their children? No, I don't. In fact, there are times when a child might actually lack capacity and capability for good and obvious reasons. However, the way such information is conveyed can foster confidence or insecurity.

Yes, most people might agree that a 2 or 3-year-old would experience a messy situation trying to hold a gallon jug of milk and properly pour milk into a cup. How this situation is handled can make a world of a difference for the child's mastery of this stage of development. Instead of saying you can't do it because you are too little, you are not big enough, you are going to make a mess; what about saying something like this: you are getting to be such a big, strong girl and you want to do some things by yourself. I think that's great! I would like to help; may I hold the jug with you and help just like you help me pick up the toys sometimes?

This is just one example of formulating your words to speak belief into the child instead of doubt. Now the child believes she can do big things. Over time, repeating this exchange can help the child develop a strong sense of self and confidence even when things are challenging. The above example also teaches the child a sense of team work. Again, repetition of such interactions prepares the child to continue growing in a healthy manner, throughout each successive stage of development.

Also, with harmonious passion; there is flexibility related to how behaviorally engaged you are. The activity, thing, or person does not control you. If there are negative psychological or relational consequences, a person with harmonious passion will become flexible and make adjustments to continue experiencing good vibes that healthy, harmonious, passion brings. Conversely, obsessive passion stems from being controlled by something or someone. Take a look.

Obsessive Passion. With obsessive passion, there is little room for flexibility. Passion drive does not stem for as internalized identity with the object of the obsession. In his research study, Vallerand also mentions his findings related *to passion and relationships, passion and performance, and passion and physical health.*

Here is an example of relationship issues that comes to mind, as associated with obsessive passion. Remember, obsessive passion is controlled by an unhealthy obsession toward a person or thing. If I have an obsessive passion associated with writing and being an author, I am more likely to disregard my relationship with my spouse when I am in my writing zone. Developing a manuscript takes time, and my spouse might be starved for my attention; yet I continue writing because I am driven to be the best author and I am focused on how successful I will be in relation to other authors. My drive to perform would lead me to inflexibility and rigidity.

Another example of obsessive passion: you identify yourself as a helper. You are driven to help people, even when helping interferes with selfcare. Although you have been driven by this passion for some time now, you often question the origin. You ask yourself, is this healthy passion or not? After a few sessions of insight-oriented therapy you discover that your desire to help others is tied to people-pleasing tendencies. You grew up in a household where you were praised when you were available for everyone's needs and desires, and you were rejected when you said no to certain requests. This repetition of behavioral patterns shaped your thought processes about what helping means.

Also associated with an obsessive passion drive is unhealthy decision-making and performance-based, competitive behaviors. For example, your spouse is very good at skating. You have not skated since you were a child. Your spouse is very competitive. You have learned that you are not as competitive. You skate with your spouse once, and you fall. You realize that you should not take on this activity and risk hurting yourself. There are way too many risks involved and you are not in the position to break any part of my body without possible long-term consequences.

Now, what if you have an obsession to prove and compete? What if you decide you will keep trying in order to keep up with your spouse? This response would align more with an obsessive, unhealthy passion. In the long-run, you are not making a healthy decision if you injure yourself. Skating is not a harmonious passion for you. You do not identify with it. You decide that you can tag along and takes pics and video your spouse while he skates. You can enjoy the music and enjoy watching others skate; and there are no risks of injuring yourself.

Based on DMP, obsessively passionate people will either engage in performance goals or performance-avoidance. What does this mean? This means that the end goal of the passion is not mastery, like those who are harmoniously passionate. The end goal is to win or succeed over others. If there is any doubt that winning will happen for the obsessively passionate person, that person will avoid the performance activity altogether. For obsessively passionate person, the inclination toward passion is in relation to others; for the harmoniously passionate person, others are not a factor. Harmoniously passionate people want to master what they are drawn to and will spend much time, over a long period of time, remaining committed to their passion because there is internalized identity attached.

Constructs That Impact Passion

Certain constructs impact passion in your life. As you review the following constructs: familial, cultural, biopsychosocial, religion, and education; in the note section at the end of this book, jot down thoughts that stand out for you.

Familial. Your family of origin has a hand in your understanding of passion. You are a part of a family environment that makes a difference in your awareness and understanding of passion. In fact, how you interacted with your family can determine your idea of passion to the extent that you are obsessively driven, or you are harmoniously driven by passion.

Think back to what you read previously about stages of development. Now consider the following examples. These are only some possible experiences that could pave the way and set the course for the type of passion you mostly align with: harmonious or obsessive passion. Let's say you grew up with siblings and there was comparison between you and your siblings. You were told that you should be more like your older brother or sister. You were regularly reminded of how good your other siblings are and you were encouraged to try harder, to be more like your siblings.

Maybe you were discouraged from certain activities, sports, or interests because you were not good enough. Perhaps you wanted to play basketball but were told you were too short, or you enjoyed football but were told you were too little or too thin. Did you want to be a model but were told you don't have the appropriate shape, height, or appearance? Were you interested in being an actor/actress, but were told you would never make it in Hollywood because you are not talented enough?

What about families of doctors, lawyers, military folks, etc.? There are times when families expect their offspring to follow in their footsteps. In therapy I have worked with individuals who struggled with doing what is important to them, because of being heavily influenced or even pressured by family toward a particular career path. From a very young age, some people have been told what field of study is best. Even if a particular idea is not forced, or modeled with expectation to follow, some individuals might assume they are expected to follow a certain path. Some individuals put pressure on themselves and conclude that the way to be accepted and loved is to do what is an assumed or real expectation; and the way to being rejected is to go against real or perceived expectations.

Additionally, there are certain families who own businesses and there is an expectation of certain family members to partake in operation of the business. When I was growing up, my dad partnered with a family and co-owned a grocery store. My dad's partner had all of his children working in the store. He opened a second location and the older of the children operated the second store. I would go to the store during summer months and soon I was being taught how to operate the cash register, do inventory, stock items, and so on. This was my first experience of seeing the expectation of keeping the family business in the family.

My mother was a stay at home mom; this is the model I saw and what I knew throughout my stages of development. She was always home and she did a good job at providing a consistent expectation when we arrived home from school. She was very predictable. When my siblings and I arrived home from school, more days than not, dinner was already done. Certain expectations were made clear repeatedly; we followed accordingly enough until following expectations became like second nature. In my thinking and desire, from the time of elementary, I was going to be a wife, a mom, and a teacher. No one knew my thoughts of what I wanted to do with my life, and no one held an expectation over my head. I now know that my thoughts were largely shaped by what I was exposed to; what I observed, that was modeled in my day-to-day. My thoughts of doing more with my life were limited because my exposure was limited.

This is a true statement in general. You will be hard-pressed to become a well-rounded, openminded person if you do not get out of your familiar zone and explore this huge world. If you are not one for extensive travel you can explore through reading and taking short road trips. You will grow and develop according to what you learn and know. Results are determined by how much you are willing to challenge yourself. Do not pressure and compare yourself to others; whatever your personality and passions are, just do not limit yourself. You might have to be more creative if you are the careful, less daring type. It is perfectly okay; no pressure. Brace yourself, as you need to; but be sure to do something that challenges you, something that gets you out of what is comfortable for you.

Cultural. If you are one who has been governed by culture because your family is steeped in cultural norms, you know what it is like to be told what to do, rather than to be allowed to flow in your own internalized passion; those things you innately identify with as valuable to *YOU*, those things that you would spend hours engaging in and still not become tired.

So, what are some challenges related to cultural constructs? Some people become emotionally and psychologically upset, and experience anxiety and depression because they feel cultural pressure that stifles and interferes with passion. Those who become emotionally and psychologically upset are actually healthy. Something within goes off as a warning sign, just as signals that show up in your car when something is going wrong or needs attention.

Pay attention to everything that is going on inside of you, you might be getting a message that you are not happy because you are not living your most passionate life. Your symptoms point to a greater problem of life dissatisfaction because you know something is missing. Whatever you do, do not ignore what is going on inside of you. Listen to the message and do something about it. Your freedom begins when you are able to assertively express your needs and develop bravery to live your passion, even if someone else does not agree. Now I am not claiming this to be an easy process. Again, how steeped in culture you or your family are will determine the degree of difficulty you might expect to interface with. But be assured, nothing changes until something changes.

Bio-psycho-social. This trifecta encompasses three parts of human beings that interplay. In my practice I conduct a biopsychosocial assessment to gain better understanding of those I serve. The following is a diagram and concepts to illustrate the biopsychosocial correlation (see *diagram 1*).

Crystal Scott, LMFT, M.A., B.S.

Biological   **Psychological**

Social

(Biopsychosocial diagram 1)

Biologically. Your biological components impact passion. For this section, it is important to understand the difference between your mind and your brain. Your brain is a part of your biological makeup and is a physical organ, your mind is not. It is said by some that *"the mind is what the brain does."* Your brain's cerebrum (the physical) is an important factor in how your thoughts, emotions, attitudes, beliefs, imaginations, and memories are translated to other areas of your body. Your brain is responsible for how your mind permeates every cell of your body. Ultimately, your mind greatly impacts your body in general.

Psychologically. This reference focuses on your conscious and unconscious mind. You need to understand the health of your 3-part psyche or your mind (your id, ego, and superego) and the health of your emotions. This understanding is necessary in order for you to adequately grasp concepts of constructs that impact passion, and ascertain how constructs interplay with functions of passion. Here we will take a brief look at the 3 parts of your psyche: *id, ego, and superego*:

Id. Your id is the part of your psyche associated with your impulses, your primitive or early stages of development, your very basic functions in early life.

When your id is in control; you generally are acting without thinking, being very impulsive.

Ego. This part of your psyche is responsible for self-identity and self-esteem. If your ego is healthy, you will not overestimate or underestimate your value. If your ego is inflated or deflated, your ego functioning is not healthy.

Superego. The superego is composed of ideals you learned from home, school, society, religious communities, etc. Your superego keeps your id in check so that your impulses do not run wild. Your superego also plays a role in keeping norms and rules, and certain socially acceptable standards; and in some ways, your superego keeps your ego in check. This part of your psyche can be viewed as the balancer between the id and the ego.

At this juncture, let's consider a danger to passion. When there is no balance and harmony among the three parts of your psyche you risk running into a brick wall and experiencing doubt and defeat. For example, if you give too much leeway to your superego and you are low on ego, watch out! Everything and everyone else will be in your head and impede your flow of passion. Also, if you are governed greatly by your id and impulses, you are more prone to obsessive passion that can be unhealthy and destructive. Don't allow impulses to guide and you. Keep your ego healthy, not overinflated or deflated, balance yourself with a healthy superego.

In sum: if your thought life is unhealthy, if you are low on emotional intelligence and high on impulses and drives; you are vulnerable to experience interruption and interference related to your passion.

Socially. Certain social factors associated with socialization and assimilation matter, as they influence passion. There are some children who grow up with a strong will that can tip over to rebellion quite easily. When these qualities are dealt with and attended to effectively, anything that comes across as a weakness can be shaped into a strength. Not necessarily changing the strong will of the child, but helping the child to use strong-will qualities more effectively.

Here is what I mean. Let's say a child tends to question everything. I know this can be frustrating, but the opposite is that the child will do whatever she is told. Now let's say the parent manages to get the child to stop questioning by whatever means of discipline or correction is used. Now the child is in social environments and the child has learned to not question, just do what is told or asked. Once this behavior is shaped, there might be times that confidence, boundaries, and a strong sense of self are no longer there for the child.

Sure, it is necessary to train children because training can help with healthy adaptation. When children are trained to conform at home, school, in the temple, mosque, or church; it is also helpful to add balance. Allow for a sense of self-awareness and self-identity. Remember, this is how healthy ego is developed. You want your child to be well-rounded. You do not want your child to be a stubborn, bullheaded know-it-all rebel; but you also do not want an acquiescent child who is mindless, and lacks confidence. Conformity, without balance, can lead to a people-pleasing, approval-seeking type of personality. This, of course, can adversely impact passion.

Religion. I am careful to make the distinction that I am not referring to spirituality here. When I speak of religion I speak in terms of those practices and beliefs that are firmly held and adhered to. Religion can adversely impact any passion you have that transgresses or goes against certain religious beliefs and practices. Go back to your reading on the superego. Do you remember that this is a part of the mind that makes up ideals that have been engrained in you as you have developed?

What you have been told and taught, time-after-time, will invariably surface in general; but such teachings will especially come into play when you consider passions that might not align with what you have been taught religiously. This is a true statement for all constructs, not only religion. I want you to consider any religious barriers you face. What are some dogmas or rules that you have been taught, that keeps you feeling stuck and dissatisfied with your life? I am not suggesting anything here except that you become aware, more knowledgeable of what is going on in and around you; and pay attention to the role of these constructs in your passionate life.

Education. Perhaps you were greatly encouraged in your family, and there are no issues related to passion in this area; but in school your teachers or friends might have discouraged you. Maybe you dated someone in school who put you down and poured water on the fire of your passion. When the aforementioned construct of education impacts and influences passion, it can be very difficult to know what you uniquely are passionate toward.

There was never any pressure on me as to what I should or could do once graduating high school, but what I saw around me served as a model and I developed certain thoughts all on my own. Which included the man providing in the home and the wife staying with the children and taking care of domestic duties.

All of these factors can be good for discipline, structure, order, conformity, and cohesiveness; but these factors leave very little room for independence and uniqueness if there is not balance. Remember, as the idiom states: you do not have to "throw the baby out with the bathwater." Consider this idiom when living your passionate life; and you can also maintain factors that are worth maintaining, as you cultivate your mind and sense of independent thinking. Keep what is useful and helpful, and determine if you have the courage to discard or revise what is no longer relevant. Modification and upgrade are not bad words. In fact, we are modifying and upgrading all the time. We upgrade our electronics, our cars, and our wardrobe. We modify or revise our homes, and sometimes we upgrade or revise our relationships.

During the era of my rearing, there was way more conformity and structure than some children would understand today; but much about my era was truly helpful. I jokingly tell my clients: my environment was strict, but it kept me out of jail and the grave. I hold dear many (although not all) of the teachings I have learned throughout life because I engage all three parts of my psyche and there is balance when I make my decisions on what I will keep, what I will revise, and what I will discard altogether.

Give careful attention to these constructs. In order to get to the top place of awareness and comfortability regarding passion, it is important to understand and remember that these constructs correlate and impact your ideology and implementation of what you possess passion for. (*See diagram 2*).

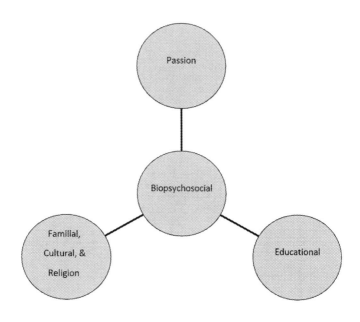

(Constructs diagram 2).

Psychological Adjustment and Overall Well-Being Are Impacted When Life Is Lived Without Healthy Passion

I am sure by now you are realizing just how intricate the concept of passion is. Passion is not only about getting the most of out life, or as Snoop Dogg and Lil Duvall Says: "Living Your Best Life;" passion is so vitally important to your overall well-being, that if your life is lived without healthy passion; your life can be adversely impacted psychologically and emotionally, as evidenced by clinical *anxiety*, and *depression*, as well as other life issues such as relationship issues, workplace issues, and even health issues.

According to the Diagnostic Statistical Manual for Mental Health (DSM 5), certain criteria must be met for individuals to be receive a clinical diagnosis. This means that you can experience certain symptoms, but not meet the full criteria to be diagnosed. For understanding of how your psychological and emotional health can be impacted when you are living a passion-filled life consider the following. Pay close attention as you read, and you will notice that some of the symptoms experienced in a stress response includes symptoms that are also experienced in anxiety and depression. Stress left unchecked or not attended to properly, can lead to complicated emotional disturbance.

Note, stress is part of life. No one escapes stress. I facilitated a training for the DFW airport recently and I addressed what it means to live a balanced home and work life. In my presentation I focused attention on the reality of stress in everything that lives. Not only do humans live with something stressful on a daily basis, so do animals, insects, and plants. Think about it, insects need to eat and they also deal with the likelihood of being crushed or swatted by humans. Animals are mistreated and abused, at times. Some live outside in horrible weather conditions, and sometimes are very stressed by hunger; in search for food. Plants and trees are beaten by brutal weather conditions as well, such as tornados, hurricanes and floods. Now, let's take a more in-depth view of the correlation between *stress, anxiety, and depression.*

Stress. Stress is your body's reaction to harmful situations; although, you also experience good stress as well (such as a new relationship, a new career, the birth of a child, etc.). However, I am addressing stress experienced as a reaction to unfavorable situations or events. It does not matter if you have actually experienced harmfulness or you have the perception that you are in harm's way. When you feel threatened, for any reason, your internal fight-or-flight system is activated. This internal system is designed to help you to cope, protect yourself, and keep yourself safe. The following are examples of symptoms you might experience when stressed. These symptoms are NOT directly quoted from the DSM 5.

- Low energy.
- Headaches.
- Upset stomach, including diarrhea, constipation, and nausea.
- Aches, pains, and tense muscles.

- Chest pain and rapid heartbeat.
- Insomnia.
- Frequent colds and infections.
- Decline in sexual desire.
- Irritability.
- Anxiety.
- Depression.
- Feeling overwhelm and a loss of control.
- Difficulty relaxing and quieting the mind.
- Low self-esteem.
- Avoiding others.
- Nervousness and shaking.
- Cold or sweaty hands and feet.
- Dry mouth and difficulty swallowing.
- Clenched jaw and grinding teeth.

Anxiety. Anxiety, according to the DSM 5, is characterized as excessive worry (apprehensive expectation), occurring more days than not for at least 6 months, about a number of events or activities such as, but not limited to work or school performance.

Individuals who experience anxiety find it difficult to control worry; anxiety and worry are associated with three or more of the following six symptoms, with at least one symptom having been present for more days than not for the past 6 months. For children to be diagnosed, only one criterion or symptom is required.

1. Restlessness or feeling keyed up or on edge.
2. Difficulty concentrating or mind going blank.
3. Being easily fatigued.
4. Irritability.
5. Muscle tension.
6. Sleep disturbance (difficulty falling asleep, staying asleep, or unsatisfying sleep).

Depression. In some cases, even depressed individuals demonstrate some form of passion. You might observe passionate expressions from individuals experiencing what is identified as agitated depression. When such individuals are aware that something is missing, and they are not living healthy passion, they sometimes demonstrate unhealthy passion outlets. Might sound unbelievable, but this is a true statement and many people are in this category, unfortunately. Instead of being subdued and immobilized by feeling depressed, these individuals are more likely to be animated. You have seen them; they are the life of the party in some cases. Oftentimes, individuals experiencing agitated depression exhibit road rage behaviors. Such individuals are more likely to engage in risk-taking activities, are always on the go, and they experience impairment in multiple life environments such as home, work, and social scenes.

There is a mathematical concept at work in the depressed mind. In the mind of individuals who live an uninspiring life without healthy passion, these individuals begin by calculating some things in their life, and some things just do not add up. Instead of good thoughts and experiences being added to their life, they feel the drain. More goes out of them; more is subtracted or taken away from them. So, how do you determine if feeling depressed is just a fleeting emotional experience that will pass, or something more serious? A depressive mood lasting for 2 consecutive weeks that includes the criteria outlined in the Diagnostic and Statistical Manual for Mental Illness (DSM 5) qualifies you for a depressive disorder:

1. Depressed mood most of the day.
2. Loss of interest or pleasure most of the day.
3. Change in weight or appetite (as significant as a 5% change).
4. Observe psychomotor (physical agitation) or rigidness.
5. Fatigue.
6. Feelings of guilt or worthlessness.

7. Difficulty concentrating or making decisions.
8. Insomnia or hypersomnia.
9. Recurrent thoughts of death or suicide, or suicide attempts.

Research suggests, if you are going to live an overall healthy life, this includes physical, emotional, and psychological well-being. When your overall life is healthy, you are equipped to live a life of healthy passions. But you do not need research to convince you. You live with *YOU* day in and day out. You are fully aware of the challenges you face when you feel as if something is missing. Some of the following statements are what I have heard in my seventeen plus years as a therapist. Below are some statements that individuals commonly say to themselves when life is not lived passionately:

- "I am not happy with my life and I don't know why."
- "I feel detached."
- "Everyone seems to be ahead of me and progressing."
- "I should be doing something else with my life."
- "I don't know what my purpose is."

- "How can I find out what I am supposed to be doing."
- "I have a degree, but not happy in the field I have chosen."
- "Some of my friends seem to have it all together and I feel left behind."
- "I am different from everyone in my family and feel like I have to act like them or I'll be treated like an outcast."
- "I don't think I have ever thought about myself; I always take care of others."
- "I am not good with boundaries; I am a people-pleaser."
- "I feel guilty or bad when I put my wants and needs above others."
- "I know I seek others' approval."

As you read the above quotes, can you relate? Perhaps you can and maybe you also have other thoughts of your own that are not a part of the list. These are very common thoughts related to people who grapple with the ideas of: what next, or what now? I remind patients that they are most healthy when they ask such questions and when they are not comfortable where they are in life. Humans are created to be creative, to thrive, and to live a passionately, thunderous life.

When life feels bland and out of sorts, this is grist for the mill that leads to query and exploration to determine: where do I go from here? Now that you have an understanding of how passion impacts your overall well-being; it is important to delve deeper. In this next section you will gain insight regarding functions of passion. Passion serves many functions. Here you will discover how passion fuels, flows, floods, and fosters.

Functions of Passion

Fuels. Passion is like a fire. You will find that I often use this concept to identify passion because the intensity of passionate feelings can be stirring and agitating, and will not allow you to rest or become lackadaisical. The fuel of passion keeps you going when you would otherwise give up and quit. When you experience the effects of harmonious passion; you are in touch with healthy energy, energy that is needed to accomplish what you are passionate about. Your life is balanced, you are in control, and you can enjoy a variety of experiences. Let's say your passion is toward a relationship.

Regardless of difficulties experienced; you have the capacity and passion to stick it out because you are passionately connected. This could explain why one person can be remain in a marital relationship with someone who is a real challenge, while any other person would end the relationship without a moment's notice. Let me be clear here. There are some people who are codependent and dysfunctionally attached in relationships, they remain in challenging relationships for unhealthy reasons. This idea aligns more with unhealthy passion.

Flows. If you do not experience flow, you are not harmoniously passionate. Just as I am free-form writing this book, September 7, 2019. I have been at it since 1 p.m. and it is now 10:20 p.m. Of course, I have had a couple of short breaks, but totally I have been at it for at least eight hours. I am flowing out of my knowledge of course, but also out of my passion for the topic.

When you are harmoniously passionate; commitment, energy, creativity, and excitement endures and flows. Becoming lost in the flow is very common. This is why I encourage you to balance your time. I tell you this because I am keenly aware of how easy it is to become stuck in a cycle of becoming lost and nothing else matters, sometimes not even food or water. But do take caution to take care of yourself as you flow.

Floods. Have you ever experienced a flood? It overtakes and overwhelms. Little by little, before anyone knows what is going on, flooding has taken over and is in complete control. Likewise, so does passion. In intense moments of your flow you are flooded with so much. If you have waited for a while to get started you might be experiencing a backup, as when someone is congested. Once medication is administered and everything opens up, your nose runs constantly.

This is an example of what flooding can look like for you when you are flowing in your passion. You do not miss a beat. You are in a flood; you are taken away and you are unhindered and unforced. Here is where you want to differentiate between harmonious and obsessive passion. When passion floods, this is good and healthy. However, when you do not add balance; flooding can be as destructive as floods that are natural disasters. If you do not implement self-care in this process; beware, you might be in obsessive passion.

Fosters. Now that you understand fueling, flow, and flooding of your passion, you must also know that passion fosters. Yes! Passion promotes a sense of psychological well-being and stimulates positive emotions that can carry into other areas of your life. Can you imagine how much better and how much more enjoyable you can be in relationships across many areas of your life when you are happily living your passionate life?

Not only are you encouraged, but you have something to offer others. You might be motivated to help others understand their passion. As you are nurtured and enriched by what brings you good vibes, you are more likely to want to help others cultivate their passion. Who knows? You begin a chain reaction of others helping others to understand passion and advance.

Certain qualities emanate from those who live passionate lives. These qualities are not manufactured. In fact, passionate people are not usually aware of how others observe and perceive these qualities; largely because the flow element is so much an intrinsic part of passionate people. Passionate people are in their natural element; they are not focused on what others might perceive. When in your flow of passion, qualities that emanate from you are your *eyes, your smile, your tone, your vibe or energy, and your presentation*:

Your eyes. Your eyes contain and convey a glow; your eyes indicate that you, and your passion are one. If you are speaking, teaching, performing, etc., your eyes tell others you are in your flow of passion. Several people have commented to me that I am pleasant as I approach them. I am sure to make eye contact. I realize this is an important quality to express to others just how important they are, and they are worthy of my respect. As a result, many individuals have seen more through my gaze; not only respect for their presence, but a passion for life.

Your smile. Similar to your eyes, that glow with passion, your smile indicates your happiness and sense of satisfaction. Let's say you are motivationally speaking about a topic or engaged in some form of entertainment or service. When you are passionate about what you are doing, it is difficult to hold back your smile. Your smile signifies that you are in your zone, in your lane; and your life is satisfied. You are confident in your competence, and you are sure you are impacting others with your passion.

This is why some people who experience life stressors can smile. They have discovered a secret. Such people live out their passion in a healthy enough manner, and they can balance challenges otherwise faced. These people are happy and their lives are psychologically and emotionally adjusted.

Your tone. Tone is another indicator. Think about it. Have you ever witnessed someone facilitating a meeting or a training? I am on both ends of the spectrum. I am a facilitator, and I am a part of the audience at time. While in the audience I have experienced facilitators who are so engaging and passionate that I am pulled into the topic, not only because of the material, but the tone, pitch, confident expression, and passionate connection arrested me; and held my attention.

I have also been in the presence of some facilitators and I wondered if they were forced to present or were presenting out of some obligation. During such times, I was easily distracted and found it a challenge to remain engaged. This is no slight to anyone; I am aware that sometimes people have an off day or two. I am simply providing examples to further your learning and understanding of both sides of the coin as related to passion qualities.

Your vibe or energy. I am aware that some people are very animated and also loaded with caffeine just to get through long, busy days. These might be the same people with high energy. But not all energy is caffeine based. Do you remember in my introduction, when I mentioned my encounter with Candace? It was an early morning for me. Let me just be honest here, anything before 10:00 a.m. is early for me. This is my reality and I have made peace with it; and I commonly share this truth very comically and candidly.

Back to my encounter with Candace. It was early morning, or should I clarify? It was early for me. By the time I spoke with Candace it was not 11:00 a.m. yet. I arrived on site before 9:00 a.m. Mind you, I had no caffeine and no breakfast. Well, I had a banana and water. Still, I had no reason to be animated or over-the-top energetic, except for the fact that I was at a book event to share my publications, and this is definitely passion for me.

I was seated when Candace began to speak to me; when she spoke to my passion. Without thinking to do so; I leaped from my seat. As Candace spoke to me, I blinked my eyes rapidly to hold back the tears. Candace told me to let it go. She said: "Don't fight it, you'll still look pretty anyway." We laughed, and continued to share. This was a moment and memory I want to remember and share for as long as I can. When passion is at work, things that would otherwise largely challenge, seem to be non-factors.

Your presentation. Presentation encompasses a lot. Including how you carry yourself outwardly and how apparent it is that you take care of yourself overall. You would be hard-pressed to find someone of a passion-filled life who does not take care of life overall. This presentation I speak of also encompasses your energy, tone, eyes, and your smile.

Think back to what I said a few sentences prior: you and your passion are one. Let's say I claim that I am passionate about living a stress-less life. I brand myself as a stress-less guru. Notice, I did not say stress-free. Life will never be stress-free, but you can stress-less. My point: if I come to you and present with a disheveled appearance, low energy, and unkempt, you might not believe I'm passionately living a stress-less life. You might begin to wonder if what I am

sharing about stressing less is even a real
possibility. Presentation matters!

This chapter has provided you with a description
of passion. As a result of reading this chapter, you not
only understand types of passion, but you also have
knowledge of how passion functions. Additionally, you
understand the importance of doing what it takes to
live psychologically healthy, as well as healthy overall.
Finally, you have knowledge of qualities demonstrated
in a passion-filled life. Now let's move on and further
your understanding as you learn how to effectively deal
with doubt.

"Go out into the world with your passion and love for what you do, and just never give up."

Dianne Reeves

Chapter II

DEALING WITH DOUBT

The first thing you need to know about doubt is this: doubt is a liar, a thief, and a murderer. At times, doubt speaks loudly; and at other times doubt speaks in a whisper. Doubt tells you negative, distorted, self-defeating things to create fear, to keep you from being courageous enough to do what you are passionate about. These lies can paralyze you and keep you stagnant. In my introduction I mentioned the importance of self-awareness. But I must also mention that a healthy sense of self is a must. You will need these qualities to overcome doubt.

Doubt is a thief that can rob you of your zeal and tenacity. You become immobilized; caught in a vortex that you cannot escape. If allowed, doubt will kill your passionate spirit, doubt will murder your drive. Like a hammer, doubt nails you to the wall of uncertainty; you second guess, and question yourself. Somehow you allow yourself to agree with doubt and it becomes you. What you do when faced with doubt is important. Act sooner rather than later. Begin immediately, and challenge any negative mindset that weighs you down with doubt. The more you linger, the more time and power you give doubt to do what doubt does: destroys and kills.

Empowering information can serve you well in moments of doubt. During my research phase of writing, I came across Milton Friesen, located in Ontario, Canada. Friesen is a life coach, among other roles. I will summarize his take on a couple of elements of passion that you might find helpful when you are faced with doubt: *your composition and your capabilities.* Empowering information can serve you well in moments doubt. Consider how you are composed; this is your central focus. Once you understand how you are composed, and who you are in personality and in relation to things that are of interest to you; then you will do well to surround yourself with individuals and environments in which you can feed your inborn qualities.

Additionally, if you take in negativity on a regular basis, you are sure to become negative and doubtful. You need people and life experiences that are conducive to your passion. You need people who not only get your personality and understand the way you are wired; but you need people who are capable and willing to be a supportive network as you continue to build and fortify yourself.

Another element Friesen mentions, is capability. Focus your attention on what you can do and not on what you cannot do. There are some things that you probably want to do and wish you really could do, but if such things are more of a limitation, you will frustrate yourself. This is not to say you should not try things that challenge you. If something matters to you, to the degree that you want to give it a try, do so. For example, perhaps you have always loved art and wanted to ultimately open your own art gallery. You have attended university, received your degree, and you began your journey of fulfilling your passion. Things did not turn out as you had hoped. You have tried everything you could imagine to try, with no success. But you really love art.

You have options. You could partner with an established art gallery, and later branch out independently. You could relocate and look at other demographical areas. I am sure there are a few other options that could keep you connected to your love for art, until you are able to ultimately achieve your passion. In the meantime, if you desire to remain in the atmosphere of art; you can teach art. However, there are times when you might have to make adjustments to what you are passionate about. In my twenties, I was very passionate about the medical field. I worked approximately six years in the field.

It was clear to me that I was not cut out for certain aspects of the medical field when I worked as a medical secretary in an emergency room, in Oakland, CA. I do not have a strong stomach and adjustments had to be made. I eventually found a way to connect with my passion as a helper in the healthcare industry. Helping people is what I love to do. Seeing people healthy and self-directed brings joy to me; and I kept at my passion until I landed in my sweet spot. Did it take some time? You bet it did. Remember, I started out in my twenties;

I did not secure my long-term place as a practitioner until almost twenty years later.

Here is what I suspect happened to me, something that I do not want to happen to you. I did not have anyone teaching me the principles I am sharing with you. I winged it along the way, and I thank God that I did not dangle much longer than I did. Do I wish I had gotten in touch with my passion sooner? Yes, I do. Do I believe that timing has hindered me in any way? Absolutely not. Although I wish I had started my career sooner, I could not because I was ill-prepared. This does not have to be your story. Hone or sharpen unique skills you currently possess; and be a forever learner of what you are passionate about. Stay around elements and environments of things you are passion about. Research and gain all the knowledge you can, as stated earlier. Connect with a supportive network of people who validate your unique composition.

Be assured, doubt is very powerful. If you do not engage in self-awareness and if you do not understand how doubt works against passion, you can be caught off guard. Without realizing, you can begin to wonder if what you are passionate about is real passion at all. The following words are synonymous to doubt: uncertain, unsure, confused, apprehensive, mistrust or misbelief, hesitance, uneasiness, and suspicion. If you can relate to any of these concepts, you are in doubt.

Imagine with me and consider the word doubt as a seed. If you struggle with doubt, the first thing you want to do is understand how you have learned to be doubtful toward yourself. Sure, you might have doubt about *something* you are passionate about; but the real issue is that you are also doubting yourself. Whatever you are passionate about requires your mind and body to express passion. Essentially, when you doubt whether or not what you are passion about can materialize, you are really questioning *your* potential to bring life to your passion.

The seed of doubt is planted and takes root the moment you accept the concept of doubt and begin to apply it to your life. Think about it, who has told you that your ideas are unrealistic? Who told you that you are taking on more than you are capable of accomplishing? At what point in your life did you agree with someone's assessment of you? When you doubt yourself there is an origin, a place and time in your life when you initially doubted your capabilities. It can be helpful for you to go back to the time when doubt began. Once you locate the earliest memory of your experience of doubt, this is the place where your greatest and toughest work of rewriting the script of your life begins.

If you have never heard of the concept of rewriting your life script, now is a good time to be introduced. When you begin to doubt yourself and your passion because of negative self-talk and because of negative things you have been told, you need to make a decision about rewriting the script you have swirling around in your head that leads to doubt. Your mind is your weapon; but at times you don't feel powerful to use your mind to defeat thoughts and words spoken to you, that have impacted your self-belief. Your new script is the counter to anything negative that you have accepted. In your new script, you no longer accept thoughts that distort your view of yourself. Today, you get to tell a different story about yourself.

When you are discouraged, deterred, and detoured by doubt you need to know what to do. The first thing you want to do is ask yourself critical questions. For example, you are passionate about being a professional athlete and you desire to play basketball for the NBA. When you were as young as you can remember, every chance you had, you kept a basketball in your hand. You played in the little league; but you did not have very many people to encourage you, except for your school coach. Your coach kept you motivated; but when you were not around the encouragement of your coach, you had to fight hard to maintain the belief that you could actually play for the NBA.

You played basketball throughout your school years up to high school, and received an athletic scholarship to play basketball at the college level; but doubt still crept in, why? During the beginning stages you needed more support and encouragement from your close circle of family and friends. This is how you are wired. You have now come to realize that your coach's encouragement alone was not enough to keep doubt from creeping in.

In this situation you have to take action. Now is the time to begin to critically examine the source of your doubt. What is your self-message that has you doubting, when clearly you have been good enough along the way to make it to the college level of basketball? Perhaps you are saying something will go wrong and you won't finish all four years, and even if you do, you are already doubting that you will be seen as good enough to play at the professional level.

Critical examination of your thoughts can make a difference at this point. Ask yourself what evidence do you have that proves you will not complete four years of college basketball and ultimately make it to pro level. If you are honest, after critical examination of your thoughts you will conclude that there is no way to possibly know how things will turn out. Then ask yourself why do you choose to question your potential as opposed to focusing on encouragement from your coach and the scholarship you are offered. Ask yourself how did you learn to think the worst possible thing would happen and not have hope and trust in yourself that you can be as good as you need to be to make it to the NBA.

Next, ask yourself what is the worst thing that could happen if you do not make it to the NBA. Here is another reality associated with passion. When you operate in your passion, you do not always know exactly what will materialize out of your passion. A shift in the way you think about passion becomes necessary at times. If you are passionate about basketball, and worst-case scenario, you are not drafted to the NBA, what is your self-message. You get to determine how you assess and evaluate the decision of others.

If you are not selected do you conclude that this confirms you were not good enough. Remember, whatever you tell yourself is your truth that you live by. The more you build concepts of doubt and live by these concepts, this becomes your automatic way of thinking and then it becomes easier to doubt yourself more and more as related to other passions and desires you have for life.

So, if you are not selected to the NBA, what could be other reasons, other than you were not good enough. If you did your best and gave it your all, can you find a way to let this be your peace? What about considering this: maybe you have gone as far as you were going to go and you completed the season of that passion. If you still have passion for the game, ask yourself if there is something else you can do to stay around the sport: sports medicine, coach college or school-aged children. If you decide you want to move on from basketball, that is okay as well. If you move on, do so with a healthy mindset and with a healthy emotional state, so you can go forth and build upon other passions. Otherwise, doubt will cripple and immobilize you; and you will be terrified to go on to the next passionate thing in your life.

Here is an issue some people face when dealing with doubt. Doubt, not properly dealt with, can lead to a misconception about passion and potential, and could ultimately result in aborting passions. What are the consequences of aborted and unrealized passions? Sadness and depression; and possibly bitterness. So, this means at times you will need to fight for your overall psychological, emotional, and even physical health; as physical complications can ensue if you allow emotional and psychological health to deteriorate. Do you remember the poem, *Harlem*, by Langston Hughes? Review a few lines below. Remind yourself to read the entire poem later.

What happens to a dream deferred?
Does it dry up
Like a raisin in the sun….
Sag like a heavy load, or does it explode?

You can call it passion unrealized; or for the sake of this poem example, you can call it a dream deferred. I am sure you get the point. Your passions are worth too much to allow doubt to deter and destroy. Don't defer your passions; they are a part of the reason you live out loud. When you doubt, you live a dull life. So, whatever is in your way; figure it out and handle it!

What's Eating You?

Commonly, the question: "what are you eating," is asked. When doubt is wreaking havoc in your life, consider what's eating you. When you are dealing with emotional and psychological distress; for sure, something is eating you. What are your thoughts about *YOU*, that you have agreed to embrace? Your words of negativity eat away at you like a sore and cause your confidence to deteriorate into doubt.

When you are down on yourself and you continue spiraling, sometimes you need to set yourself apart and engage in self-examination. Conduct a critical examination of your thoughts to determine if there are others ways to state your claim. Reframe self-disparaging comments that bring doubt crashing down on you, impacting your self-esteem; and stifling your ability to experience passion. Take a look at a few distorted thinking processes you might need to confront and change:

Distorted Thinking

- **All-or-Nothing Thinking.** With this distortion individuals tend to think in extremes. Things are either all good or all bad. This is sometimes called black or white thinking.

   Example: If you will be successful, your parents have to be successful. If boys are going to be confident, they have to be raised by their father.

This kind of thinking does not leave room for any exceptions or other possibilities. These are probably some people's experience, but not all.

- **Overgeneralization.** Individuals who overgeneralize will apply one life experience to all areas of life.

  Example: A man who has been in a relationship with several women who have been unfaithful says: "all women cheat."

- **Mental Filter.** In this example, thoughts are minimized or maximized. In a given situation, if the possibility of a positive outcome exists the possibility would be minimized and the negative would be maximized.

  Example: Although she is doing well in her studies, and she has been told she has an opportunity to receive a scholarship for college; she is one among many and there is no guarantee. The student focuses on the fact that there is no guarantee, and she speaks doubt.

- **Jumping to Conclusions**. Involves mindreading and assuming without evidence.

  Example: A coworker is the only one on her team without a degree; she thinks others do not value her input, although she is an equally active team member and there is no evidence to support her thoughts.

- **Emotional Reasoning:** When situations are interpreted and governed by feelings.

  Example: After being ridiculed and openly humiliated by her senior high school teacher, a student desires to go on to college; but her emotions rule and she becomes anxious. Believing she will be ridiculed and humiliated again, she does not apply for college.

- **Should Statements.** This includes a demanding kind of thought process. With this distortion, there is not room for anything to be done except for what individuals think and believe "should" be done.

Example: The idea that people "should" respect others. There is no way to enforce this, so to make this a "should" statement will always lead to frustration when people are not respectful.

- **Labeling or Mislabeling.** Applying one characteristic of a person and viewing the persons whole life based on that one characteristic.

    Example: This is common regarding infidelity. Someone might say that the unfaithful person is not a good person. During such times it is good to explore other aspects of the unfaithful person's character. In doing so, the injured person can separate the isolated event of infidelity that has been done; and realize there are some good things the person has done.

- **Personalization.** When exhibiting this distortion, individuals are taking things personally, as if there is a direct hit or attack aimed at them.

> ***Example:*** Someone says to a stay-at-home mom: "It's good that you get to stay home with your kids and you enjoy it. I could never do it, I tried; but felt unproductive." The stay-at-home mom says: "So you think I am unproductive!"

As you might have noticed while reviewing distorted thinking, certain styles of thinking can interplay and overlap. Such as in the examples of ***overgeneralizing***, ***jumping to conclusions***, and ***all-or-nothing*** thinking. These display similar characteristics.

Additionally, when individuals' thoughts are distorted, these thoughts can lead to emotional discomfort such as anxiety and/or depression. Once emotions are in the driver's seat (so-to-speak), distorted thoughts continue, such as what I have identified in the ***emotional reasoning*** example.

With examples of distorted thinking fresh in your thoughts, try this: In the back of your book there is a notes section. List the statements below and identify which of these you think are rules, assumptions, facts, or opinions. Consider how these relate to distorted thinking. NOTE: depending on your experiences, you might consider some statements as being rules, assumptions, and opinions. These three are subjective.

It is usually easier to distinguish facts. Facts are as clear as the following statement: ***roses are different colors***.

- I'm not good enough.
- Sugar is sweet.
- People should stop frustrating me.
- I'm lazy.
- Saying ***NO*** to someone is the same as being mean.
- My performance evaluation included some "does not meet expectations."
- Because my evaluation has some "does not meet expectations" my boss is trying to get rid of me.
- My spouse yelled at me and then stopped talking to me.
- I'm not attractive.
- I give respect, I ought to get it in return.
- People don't care about what I need.
- I did not get the promotion.
- It's not okay to disagree with my parents, regardless of my age. They know what's best.
- If I am just sitting around, I am being unproductive, there is always something I could be doing.
- You need family, they will be there for you when no one else will.

- She is not good enough for him.
- Most people my age are doing better than I am doing.
- My co-worker said she would rather not have lunch with me.
- If I do a favor, I expect one in return if I need it.
- Something will go wrong with my school project.
- The boss said I may leave work early.
- Family is important, so you should try to get along.

I trust this has been an eye-opening experience for some and a refresher for others. If you ever find yourself in a stuck place and you are not thinking as a healthy person, if your thoughts are distorted and you are driven by negative emotions; pause for a moment. Take inventory of what is going on inside of you, and around you.

In my book about depression, How Can I Laugh When Nothing's Funny? I included an acronym *H.A.L.T.* This acronym can prove helpful and useful when you are worn with doubt. Utilize these principles to help with effective selfcare and with being proactive; by developing a healthy mindset and effectively addressing distorted thinking and overcoming doubt.

H- A- L-T

This acronym is used in alcoholics anonymous (AA) to help individuals with awareness regarding lifestyle choices that could potentially lead to relapse. Individuals are encouraged to "halt," to pay attention and engage in mindfulness, to avoid potential stress that might lead to relapse.

Alcoholics anonymous (AA) teaches individuals to learn what to do when *hungry, angry, lonely, and tired.* I too have taken the "halt" position to teach you how to address certain thinking that lead to doubt. The wording has been changed a bit, as befitting for the context of this writing. *Know what to do when you become too hurried, agitated, lonely, or tired,* so that you won't relapse into doubt.

Hurried

When you are too much in a hurry you can miss out on a lot of important things in life. Take your time. Of course, there are times in life when time is of the essence; whether it is due to poor time management or due to unforeseen circumstances that put you in a bind and forces hurriedness. However, do your best to plan well and manage time effectively to minimize the possibility of being hurried.

Here is an example of what I mean when I say you can miss out on a lot being in a hurry. Think of travel, if-you-will. If you choose to travel by plane, for sure you will get to your destination much more quickly than if you were driving, that is if all goes well with your flight. However, when you are in the air there are lots of things, places, and scenery that you miss out on. When you are driving, or when you are on a bus or train, you are at a much slower pace; but you get to experience and take in so much more. With ground travel, you get to stop and smell the roses, should you decide. You get to take up-close photos of places and things to serve as memoirs of your journey. Consider it or not, but these moments are all a part of your life experiences. So, remember, don't be too hurried!

Agitated

Life will invariably present opportunities for agitation to arise. There are times when you absolutely cannot foresee agitation coming on, and before you know it you are deep in agitation. Reflect back on the previous point about being hurried, can you imagine how hurriedness can lead to agitation? It certainly can. Make it your goal to live a well-balanced stress-less life. You will never be free of stress, as life is filled with good and bad stress.

But you can live a life of less stress when take the time to plan and manage your life and relationships.

Lonely

Loneliness can be a real trigger that can lead to depression. Oftentimes, you might not realize that the well of your life is empty due to being lonely. Humans are not meant to be without relationships of some sort. If you are not in a significant relationship, if you live alone; keep something alive around you. If it is plants, goldfish, a pet; whatever it is, life around you can make a difference. Just note: healthy relationships are what you will need in order to minimize stress that can lead to depression. If you are engaging in toxic relationships, your well will be drained of the freshness and vitality you need to experience well-being.

Tired

Being too tired can also be draining. Get proper rest and relaxation. Good sleep hygiene is vital to your overall well-being and functioning, but relaxation is important as well. During your awake moments, be sure that you know what to do to relax yourself. Engage all of your senses and taste healthy and tasty snacks, breathe into your nostrils, scents that are calming, listen to something soothing or comical (get a good belly laugh), handle what feels relaxing to touch; and finally, focus your gaze on scenery, or pics, or images that are lighthearted and add to your smile.

Now that you have tools in place to address doubt, use them. Think critically and take time to pause and implement effective self-care as needed. Do not treat this pertinent information as those who look into a mirror, walk away, and forget what they look like. Read and reread this material until you create new neural pathways in your brain and become the kind of thinker who is prepared when doubt creeps in.

Principles of understanding and dealing with doubt have been delineated and I am sure these principles are imprinted in your mind. You have been provided insights, tools, and strategies to encourage and reinforce yourself; so that you will remain sturdy and steady when waves of doubt begin to roll in. What you do with this information will make a difference in your pursuit of connecting with and unleashing your passion. Now that you are prepared to deal with doubt, you are ready to dive into challenges you will face.

*"Every great dream begins with a dreamer.
Always remember, you have within you the
strength, the patience, and the passion to
reach for the stars to change the world."*

Harriet Tubman

CHAPTER III

OVERCOMING CHALLENGES

When unleashing an unstoppable passion, you will face challenges to overcome. Overcome you must, and overcome you will; If you don't allow yourself to get caught in the web of doubt. Overcoming challenges (1) requires a network of likeminded people: examples from others who have dealt with doubt and challenges to passion, and have overcome. You need to hear stories of victories and successes, you also need to hear how others might have been put down for a long time by doubt, but eventually got back up and conquered doubts and challenges. Also required is an understanding of how life and passion are impacted by modern times (2). Finally, perseverance to prevail (3) is needed, in order to realize your passions.

A Network of Likeminded People

Have you ever initiated or were assigned (against your better judgment) to work with someone on a project and the experience was excruciating? Have you ever been in a relationship (THAT YOU CHOSE) and you realized the fit was not there? I liken such experiences to this: imagine a house that is being wired. It takes precision and know-how or skill to get the job done proficiently. I am sure you already know what the risks are when skill and precision are lacking.

Okay, now let's bring this point up close and personal. Humans are uniquely wired in character, personality, and communication style. If you, are in a relationship with someone and the wiring between the both of you negatively crosses, I want you to tell me just what do you think will happen. You got it! You will not get the best out of that experience. Being in healthy relationships requires knowledge, and relational and communication skills in order to get the most and best from said relationships.

Tie this example in with living your life in a passionate way. If you are driven by harmonious passion and you are wired with someone who is driven by obsessive passion…well, good luck with that. It takes a lot to be in relationships in general, aside from all the other intrinsic intricacies we deal with as relational creatures. Sometimes we war with others, and there are times we war with our *SELF.*

No one "is an island entire of itself," according to John Donne; Thus, you will need people sometimes. Be sure to make healthy selections. Being yoked, emotionally and physically, with someone who does not respect your passions can hold you back. Check your circle of friends and associates; and evaluate what changes you need to make, based on what you need to live your most passionate life. Try as you might; if people do not desire to change, you can't change them. Since you can't change your circle, sometimes you have to change your circle. This statement is not a typo. I am indicating that you cannot change people; but you can adjust relationships within your circle, if dynamics are not healthy. I am not suggesting that you have to get rid of all your challenging relationships. If you decide to keep individuals around you who drain your energy and stress you out, have a good recovery plan. Establish ways of taking care of yourself so the impact of draining relationships does not thwart your passion.

Modern Times and Discontentment Impact Passion

In my book on depression, I address the correlation between modernity and depression. Research has been conducted and highlights modern day experiences and conveniences such as the ease of a sedentary lifestyle, more work-from-home careers, modern technology, and the way in which relationships are formed currently, versus prior times. Today, we have every convenient way of living available, but has this led to a lack of cohesiveness and connection with others? We have more and we seem to be more discontent. World Health Organization (WHO) indicates more than 300 million individuals were diagnosed as depressed and anxious in 2012.

Discontentment can lead to depression for sure. I refer you back to chapter one, under the depression heading of this reading. As I outlined depression symptoms; one symptom is a loss of pleasure or enjoyment of activities. When you lose pleasure in activities, how can you enjoy a passionate life? You will need to deal with what is discontenting you.

If you entertain the idea that certain aspects and conveniences of our modern world keep people more disconnected, then is it fair to say there is something about the synergy of healthy relationships that could add to contentment and ability to access passion? If this is a fair statement; is there also a probability that passion and healthy relationships are, in some ways, correlated?

Listen, you cannot know everything. For sure, you will not always make decisions or choices that you will like, share, or give a smiley emotion or a thumbs up to. But the more you are mindful; and the more you engage in effective decision-making strategies, the greater your likelihood of avoiding some pitfalls and also avoiding interference with your feel-good vibe and harmonious passion. Do you have to surround your entire life with likeminded people in order to stay focused and balanced as a harmoniously passionate person? The short answer is no, you do not. However, I want you to realize challenges you are more likely to face, (not guaranteed) but more likely to face; when you are surrounded with people who do not understand what it means to be you, and who do not respect how you are passionately wired. Now on to point number three. Not only do you need connections with a network of like-minded people, and an understanding of how modern times can lead to discontentment and interfere with passion; you also need perseverance to prevail.

Perseverance To prevail

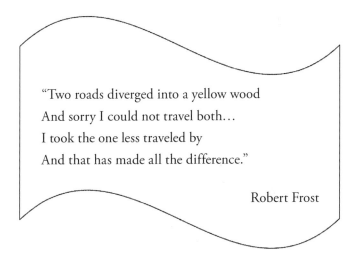

"Two roads diverged into a yellow wood
And sorry I could not travel both…
I took the one less traveled by
And that has made all the difference."

Robert Frost

You can position yourself to persevere and prevail, to develop a sense of stick-to-itiveness in the face of opposition and criticism. However, you will need to know some things about what you are up against when you go against all odds to live passionately. Not only will you come face-to-face with others who oppose you, try to throw you off course, or simply discourage you; you will also contend with *YOU*. You are a very complex being, as all humans are. Life can throw you curve balls like you could not imagine. It takes a lot to live a passion-driven life. Those who are truly, harmoniously passionate can experience great difficulty and emotional and psychological suffering because their passion is so strong, and some people refuse to walk away and abandon passion.

My encouragement and exhortation to you is this: guard your passion by staying emotionally and psychologically healthy. This means detox your mind and emotions regularly. Exercise and eat nutritiously, sleep, rest, laugh often, and play spontaneously. Be well! Treat your passion like a baby who depends on you for nourishment and sustenance. Make an oath with yourself today:

- I vow to practice positive actions on purpose, toward myself and toward others.
- I make a vow to enjoy spontaneous playfulness and to laugh often.
- I will face adversity with a healthy outlook.
- When negative vibes are around me, I will remain optimistic.
- When I am afraid, I will speak courageously to myself.

- If I am provoked to respond in an unkind manner, I will choose love.
- Bitterness and resentment must go.
- I vow to seek opportunities for growth in my challenges and conflicts.
- Adversity will become my university for lessons to learn, I will transform problems into strength.

Discipline and Balance

Discipline keeps you on course and works with you to help with maintaining focus. When you are disciplined you are more likely to structure your life in such a way that you display effective boundaries. What I mean by this is, all too often some individuals will begin a direction toward their passion and lack discipline to aid in efficacy of their set plan. Lacking discipline throws them off and then they begin to doubt whether or not their passion was true. Ultimately, these individuals end up depressed for not taking their passion seriously in the first place; and become discouraged and frustrated about possibly having to reset, start over, and establish a disciplined life. As I have said throughout this reading, real passion never goes away. You either deal with it effectively, or the consequences of not dealing with passion becomes a depressing issue in your life.

I have discussed discipline, but balance is the other factor. If you have all discipline and no balance you are more likely to neglect self-care of certain areas in your life. Believe it or not, without balance some people become so engrossed with their passion they do not eat properly, sleep properly, relax properly, and play properly. Some people also begin neglecting other people who need them, such as their partner, children, family, and so on. For further elaboration of this point, consider experiences you encounter with your computer.

You need a certain amount of bandwidth and speed to get the most out of your internet experience. This is true for your life as well. How much can you really juggle? Is it wise to push yourself to your very limit and fill your day to the full? If you do so, is there room left for effective self-care? Self-care includes being balanced and disciplined you know? You are more likely to remain keenly aware of your true passion when you leave room and space in your life for *me* time, and time for *others*. You need alone time to think and process, to reflect and meditate. Your creative juices can flow a lot smoother when you are not cluttered in your thoughts and emotions.

Back to the computer. What about too many downloaded apps, viruses, and other useless data saved on your computer? These things take up too much space and interfere with optimal use of your computer and other devices. Often, I will receive a message on my phone that I should free up space or storage on my phone or I might experience difficulty with taking pictures, videoing, downloading, and other needful functions.

Additionally, with your computer and in your life; you must possess a mindset of discipline to bypass popups and offers that can distract you from whatever tasks are in front of you. It can be very easy to get caught up in distractions if you click on that one thing, that leads to another, and yet another. Before you realize it, you have gotten completely off task. Now do this repeatedly. After a while you will feel frustrated about a dull life that is not lived passionately, because distractions can prevent perseverance.

Do you have the bandwidth to divide yourself in many different ways and still remain mindful and in tune with your passion? Of course you don't! Passion requires time and attention, focus, and diligence. Think about passion like being pregnant. When a woman conceives, let's call her pregnancy her passion. She has no idea what the child will look like, or sound like, or what the personality and temperament will be like. All the woman knows is conception has taken place. Some mothers are very concerned during the first three months of their pregnancy because the first three months are most critical and miscarriage is usually a concern. Some women have told me that they hold off announcing their pregnancy until after three months into their pregnancy.

As with pregnancy, when passion is conceived, an overwhelming and unbelievable attachment happens. What has been conceived in the heart, mind, and spirit can be unexplainable and inconceivable to the person who bears the passion, as well as to those with whom passion is shared. Nonetheless, the process has begun. You carry around your passion like a pregnant woman. You have an idea conceived in your mind, although you cannot fully determine the outcome. You could supersede your highest expectations, or you could overestimate your outcome. What is important here is to appreciate each moment, each stage, and each piece of the process; because everything, each and every nuance and detail involved is a part of you.

Let's go back to the pregnant woman. Once she gives birth, the baby might have eleven fingers and nine toes, does the mother say this is not her baby, because mom and the baby's father both have ten fingers and ten toes? Does the mother say: if anything about this child is remotely different from what I wanted and imagined; I don't want this child? I don't think so. The mother and the child are one, this is her passion she has been waiting to materialize. This is the moment she has been waiting for.

Whatever adjustments or shifts in her thinking that are needed, the mother makes the adjustments because her passion has finally been realized. She has given birth to what she has been carrying. The months were not all easy or fun, but she kept her gaze and focus on the expected end. Her body has been stretched in every way imaginable, but none of this matter. The mother also made lifestyle changes to ensure the best possible results, while her passion was being developed in utero up until the moment of her baby's entry.

The healthier the mother is, the greater the likelihood that her baby will be healthy as well. What I mean is this: mothers who desire a healthy pregnancy experience, a healthy birth, and a healthy delivery must do what is healthy. When I speak of healthy, I speak of healthy in every way. The mother will do well to think healthily, emote in a healthy manner, manage stress well, make healthy food and beverage choices, establish healthy sleep hygiene, exercise as appropriate, and implement a good skin care regimen.

This is also true for you. You cannot afford to live averagely. You are carrying precious cargo. There are brilliant and momentous ideas and possibilities within you. I know that living a passionate life with discipline and balance is difficult. Sometimes you might feel left out, because you are preserving yourself differently. It takes a lot to turn down functions or social events to stick to your commitment of discipline. Sure, you will have many moments to socialize; but when you are in a passion zone, with production deadlines; you might not be able to fit in some events. In fact, I am sure you will not; but it's okay. This is what it means to discipline and balance yourself. The following healthy behaviors are designed to further your understanding and to support you as you are garnering tools for a life of passion.

Healthy Behaviors

When you nurture passion, you will do well to implement healthy behaviors in your overall life as well. This includes your thought life, relationships, emotions, and decision-making.

Thought life. A healthy mindset is necessary and important to how you deal with passion in life. If you are prone to negativistic thinking, your thoughts impact your perception, perspective, and presentation. Although you might be passionate about something and perhaps sharing your passion with others; the way you convey your passion, based on your thought life, could adversely impact those with whom you share your passion. I have encountered many passionate people, who are confident and competent when in their passion element; but their delivery and presentation of attitude spoke volumes about their thought processes. Maybe I caught them at a not-so-good place in a moment; however, their presentation overshadowed what could have been an otherwise great experience.

Relationships. If you entertain energy draining, toxic relationships; your passion can become distressed. Your feel-good, fiery vibe can be doused by negativity and heaviness of unhealthy relationships. Here is where you want to consider what boundaries are necessary to deal with relationships that subtract from your focus and passion. Do you disconnect altogether or do you put good enough space between you and such relationships so that you are not on an emotional rollercoaster, trying to maintain and balance relationships that work against you. Which bring us to our next point about emotions.

Emotions. Because passion is a fueling, driving force; you will need your emotions to be in a healthy state. For example, let's say you are a motivational speaker. This is one area of passion for you. You are good at it and wherever you go you are sure to have thousands in the audience. You have developed a reputation and people will come from near and far to sit at your feet and experience your motivational talks. But you are stressed in other areas of your life, and your emotional health is suffering. Sure, you have been doing pretty good for a while, but stress is now taking its toll on you. The likelihood of your passion flowing through continuously has become compromised. Yeah, some people are really good at wearing a mask; but for how long? Keep your emotional life in balance and healthy.

How do you do this, you might ask? First you recognize unhealthy situations and how your thoughts are impacted. If your thoughts are negative and self-defeating; negative emotions will follow. Over a period of time, if emotions linger and do not improve; a negative mood follows. Now you are grumpy, condescending, and jaded. Although you are passionate about what you do, freely enjoying your passion becomes a real challenge (such as the example I provided under the "thought-life" heading). So, recognize what is going on sooner rather than later. This skill requires self-awareness. Which means you cannot become so busy that you do not take time to add balance to your life. Do you remember self-care I discussed earlier? Don't forget this.

Self-care is vital to the flame of your passion staying lit. Take care of your body and mind. Find relaxing strategies and activities to enjoy with others. But be assured; you also need awake time alone, doing absolutely nothing. You need time to sit with yourself, to think, reflect, meditate, assess, evaluate, and reevaluate yourself. It is always a good rule of thumb to be in tune with yourself to the end that you are knowledgeable of what you need in order to thrive and be your best. It is important to know your triggers and your hotspots. Also, keep a plan in mind of how you are going to engage in effective coping with yourself and with others. A good coping plan might include establishing a trusting relationship with a family member, friend, or a professional counselor if necessary; someone to help keep you accountable and true to the person you want to be, so you can continue to thrive in your passion.

Decision-making. Finally, good decision-making is necessary as related to passion. You might be all over the place and excited about many things. However, taking on too much and not narrowing down and fully engaging time with *something,* can lead to *nothing;* except frustration and burnout. For example, I was in the process of publishing two books, working on a video library, and I got this inkling to start a podcast. At this point, I am shaking my head. What was I thinking? I will a make a long story short.

The podcast did not last beyond two publishings. I enjoyed the information I shared, but was not at all excited about the production details needed to disseminate information podcast style. This is definitely not my passion; unless I am a guest speaker for someone else. The reality of what I had to do to maintain the process did not appeal to me at all. I stopped over a year ago and never looked back. This is how I know it is not my passion.

Make good decisions. But before you can do so, it is important to understand your current decision-making style. If you discover you do not find your current decision-making style as a strength or healthy for you, you can begin the work of developing healthy decision-making strategies. Again, if you find that you are stuck and need to talk it out, find a trusted person who is a capable of helping you locate the answer that is already within you.

Decision-Making Styles

Rational based. In this example, you use an approach that is based on logic and what is reasonable. You might delay making a decision until you are really clear about what is going on, and what the outcome will be. The drawback of this style is the likelihood of procrastination settling in. Oftentimes you can become bogged down in what has been called the paralysis of analysis. You might become stuck and stifled with all your logic and reason, and find it difficult to come to any conclusion. The upside to this style is you could avoid possibly becoming to impulsive and making rash decisions.

Impulse based. Speaking of impulsive, this style involves a gut reaction. You are more likely to be in your emotions when you make a decision. Remember this, emotions are tricky and fleeting. Have some people made emotional decisions and things turned out fine? Sure! However, you want to decide if it is okay for you to make this your primary style of decision-making. In general, an emotion is experienced when you really want to do something; it makes sense that you might be tempted to leave your brain for a moment and make an irrational decision. Just be careful to know that impulsive decision-making can be risky.

Data based. Are you a person who has to research and gather data before you decide? There is definitely nothing wrong with information. In fact, I use what is called an informed consent that is provided to patients for therapy treatment. The form has information about my practice and what can be expected. Much detail is added so that individuals can make an informed decision on whether or not they want to choose me as their therapy provider. The drawback here is that too much data can become overwhelming. You can experience decision-making constipation.

Spiritual based. How you relate to this style will depend on what spirituality means to you. Because people have different experiences with this concept, I will say here: whatever spiritual practices you engage in such as your religion or meditation, etc.; these qualities will be utilized to help with decision-making if you take the spiritual-based route. Some people have told me they burn sage or incense to clear the air of negative energy so they can relax and think more effectively, and this is their spiritual practice. Others have told me they pray and have faith; and they receive answers and direction on the path to take. There are also others who have said, in their quiet and meditative state, they have received a sign as to what decision to make. Again, this area is specific to what you believe and rely on for direction and decision-making.

Team based. A certain level of trust is needed if you are going with the team-based approach. The first thing I would have you consider is that a team can be family, friends, co-workers, or whomever. With this approach, you have decided that you are not going to only consider what you need when deciding, you are going to consider the perspective of others who will be impacted. Back to the statement of trust; if you deal with mistrust you might be leery of this approach. You might also be apprehensive to hear what others have to say, for one reason or another. Therefore, another decision needs to be made. Do you address your trust issues, or just choose not take the team-based approach? The choice is yours.

Costs/benefits based. With cost-benefits analysis you are basically weighing the pros and cons. Here lately, I have been expanding this concept with patients. So, we itemize the pros and cons, and let's say there are 4 pros and 2 cons. Now consider this: what if the 4 pros are important, but minimally important compared to the 2 cons. For example, you are deciding on a job change. The pros are increased salary, work from home, opportunity for advancement/promotion, and you get to build on your current skills that are related to your degree. The cons are you are required to be accessible by cell phone after work hours, and you are required to travel (out of town once per month, and out of the country twice per year).

The pros seem to be a good fit and the pros outnumber the cons. Although the cons are few in number compared to the pros, the cons carry much more weight. You have young kids; so, traveling often won't work for you. Also, you imagine your marriage and family will begin to experience tension and problems because of the requirement to be accessible by phone after work hours. You see, numerically the pros outweigh the cons, but experientially the cons carry more weigh and as result the pros pale in comparison.

Note: as I reference decision-making related to passion, I am not speaking in terms of deciding if you will follow your passion; I am speaking in terms of how you go about structuring and ordering factors and relationships in order to experience the best from your passion.

I would be remiss if I don't share my experiences of being challenged. Enduring times of not feeling my best and when in doubt, I first remind myself of prior points of reference when I was able to overcome challenges. When dealing with turbulent processes, I sometimes close my eyes and hold on tightly to myself as if on a roller coaster ride. Sure, I feel the scariness of it all, all the uncertainty and lack of assurance. But I still have faith that I will be okay, someway and somehow. I'm fully aware that I will not be subdued regardless of challenging experiences. I encourage myself with these words: you have gotten on this ride, and you will complete the process. Through the ups and downs, the starts and stops, and motions that seem horrifying at times; my mantra is this: I'm good and I got this!

Have I always been this kind of thinker, no I have not? Through much experience and much practice, I have cultivated and sculpted this mindset. I made this a firm decision and way of life when I grew tired and weary of being controlled by doubt and challenges. You have just been schooled about overcoming challenges. You are ready for examples of what passion unleashed and unstopped looks like. I know you will enjoy examples provided in the next chapter.

"My mission in life is not merely to survive,
but to thrive and to do so with some passion,
some compassion, some humor, and some style."

Maya Angelou

Chapter IV

PASSION UNSTOPPED

When I consider passion unstopped, I think of passion on steroids, which reminds me of times of the year when I greatly suffer with allergy symptoms. During these times my doctor prescribes prednisone, a steroid that helps with my allergy symptoms and complications. When I take the medication as prescribed, I notice I am much more energetic and can get things done more effectively. For sure my symptoms clear up fairly quickly. But what I also have noticed is the difference I feel when I have completed my medication. I feel the after effect of being irritable, groggy, and sometime lethargic or sluggish.

The experience is similar when passion is lit, and then there is an interruption. Regardless of the source of the interruption, you know when you are not in touch and in tune with your passion. Whatever served as your spark or boost has gone and you feel limp. Your inspiration and motivation might be gone, as well as your creativity. Now take inventory. What have you changed? What were you doing that worked, supported your passion, and spurred you on, that you might have gotten away from? You understand the role of doubt, and the reality of challenges as related to passion. As you persevere and prevail, you fortify yourself to experience unstopped passion; but persevering and prevailing will not just happen; you will need to exert energy and effort. Sometimes, you will need to remind yourself of this acronym: ***P.U.S.H.***

Passion. Passion is persistence inside of you that screams out like a crying infant at 3 a.m. It won't let you sleep without giving it attention. Your innate inability to resist what you are drawn to, serves as a call to action. This call to action keeps you in flow with your passion. Wherever your passion is directed, you love it, you value it, and you cannot imagine not having it in your life.

When doubts creeps in and even settles in at times, remind yourself to push.

Unleashed. Once you know passion, you can never unknow it. You are it, and it is you. You internalize and identify so much with your passion, that you do not recognize your truest, passionate self when you are disconnected from your elements of passion. Something about you seems odd, off, and out of place. Even in the face of adversities, when you are dealing with difficulties; allow your passion to remain unleashed; whatever you do, do not tether your passion. Life can be challenging enough, and sometimes even more so when you live a life of passion. Regardless, do not bind your passion. You need it to remind you of your most authentic self.

Starts. That's it! Keep the word start in mind. This means you keep starting because passion is never-ending. Passion can take you in many, many directions. You are multifaceted and amazing, so live this truth passionately. Remain unhindered and unstoppable when you start, and certainly unrestricted. If you become mundane, bland, and stale; start again. Use fresh eyes, fresh, ears, fresh thoughts, and restart. As you move about, discover something new and different that connects with your passion, and start. Master it, use it, share it; then head in another direction and repeat.

Here. Here, is wherever you have an opportunity to demonstrate your passion. Whatever place you are in currently; this is your here. When you go from that place and arrive at another, this is your here. You are limitless, boundless, fluid, and capable. Refuse to restrict yourself. When you notice you are bored and routinized in life; endeavor to discover another place for your passion to flourish, and push.

I will share with you a couple of experiences that you might remember viewing, and can possibly relate to when you think of passion. These experiences embody what I am illustrating when I say *PUSH*. The first experience is the movie "The Pursuit of Happyness," In this film actor, Will Smith and his biological son Jaden, who also played his son in the movie, went through a great ordeal. Based on a true story about a man named Chris Gardner, Will Smith stars as the character of a man very passionate about his ability to sell bone density scanners and ultimately achieve happiness.

As you recall, do you remember scenes of tears? Do you remember when I said passion is derived from the Latin word passio, which means to suffer. This story is a great example. The character felt so intensely about his capability and mastery of finally selling his bone density device. He did not stop because passion does not stop. Passion drives. Do you remember the scene when he was up in the night while his son was asleep? He was driven by the belief that he would fix the scanner and get it into the right hands.

As you think about this example, you recall all the drama and unimaginable situations he and his son were in. Is this an example of harmonious passion or obsessive passion? One might argue one way or another. I don't perceive the character as obsessed, I don't know that he had a lot of options; but he had passion. Also, remember this; obsessive passion must present with an unhealthy quality of taking risks for the sake of competition and performance. This character was trying to survive. He also really believed in his capability to be a good salesperson, and to give his son a good life.

My next example is the movie "Acrimony". A film by Tyler Perry. Taraji P. Henson plays the wife of a man who believes in his battery invention. Was this harmonious passion or obsessive passion? Certainly, he put his wife through a lot, but motives matter. Did he really believe he had it in him to make up for all the loss and pain he caused her? It certainly appeared so. As with the example of "The Pursuit of Happyness," there was no indication that either of these men were ruthlessly dismissing others in their lives to compete and take risks because of being controlled by obsession. These examples of drive were to better their conditions; and also benefit their families.

In "Acrimony," just as in "The Pursuit of Happiness," both of these men stuck to their passion. The spouse in "Acrimony" worked arduously through many years, causing tension in his home; and his marriage ultimately ended. He wanted his marriage, but he needed his wife to believe in him. She gave many years and lots of money; ultimately, she concluded she had nothing left to give.

One more example is an all-time favorite of mine. The Rocky movies. I can watch these movies over and over. I never tire of watching them and I discovered why. These movies speak to passion for me. I am not a person who will repeatedly watch movies. I do not buy DVD movies because, as I said; I do not repeatedly watch movies. However, if I walk into a room and Rocky is on, I am halted. It does not matter if it is Rocky I or Rocky IV, I am all in. I have memorized many of the scenes and words; Rocky never gets old for me. Why? Because passion does not get old for me.

I was searching my blogs and came across an entry from April, 2019. The title was: "Passion Prevails." Seeing this entry sparked my passion to write this book even more. My entry was entered as a result of sitting on my couch one Saturday afternoon watching television and a Rocky marathon was on. This is how my entire Saturday was spent. If you know anything about Rocky; he was determined. Rocky started out as a street kid. The odds were against him. From all appearances his destiny was sealed and things were not looking good for him. Rocky did not have a lot materially, and he was not academically sharp. However, Rocky was relational and simple. Rocky held passion for Adrian and for boxing. Rocky also held passion for family and friend relationships.

Do you remember early on, when I discussed the role of healthy relationships in your life? Consider Rocky's relationship with Adrian. They both held passion for each other. He gained strength and energy because she remained a positive presence and support, even when she was afraid and did not understand his commitment to boxing. Their passion for one another helped with passion in other areas of their life. Passion leads to passion. It grows, flows, spreads like a wildfire; and it floods.

I told you I remember many scenes and words from Rocky. One that stood out for me while watching in April, is one I'll share with you. Rocky promised Adrian he would stop boxing. She was pregnant and she was afraid of his boxing lifestyle. Rocky decided to let go of the street life and his old ways of earning money, in order to focus on his new life with his wife and soon to be child. Rocky found a job with his brother-in-law, butchering meat. It was not long before he was told that business was slowing down; Rocky was let go. Last hired, first fired. Rocky found his way back to the boxing gym. He asked his trainer, Mickey, if he could do some work around the gym. Rocky did not seem to mind; just as long as he was back in his element of passion, even if he was not in the capacity of a boxer.

While there in the gym, Rocky's job was to empty spit buckets, clean up, and sweep. Others around the gym recognized him as a fighter, a champion. Rocky was teased and belittled, and talked about because he was now cleaning up after other boxers who were training. Mickey did not like what he saw Rocky doing. Rocky pretty much begged Mickey saying: I just need to be around it, even if I am not fighting." As you recall information you have read in previous chapters, this example should make previous learning a little more clear.

Long story short, Rocky was repeatedly called out by Apollo Creed and this frustrated Rocky and Mickey. Mickey encouraged Rocky to fight again. While Adrian was upstairs, Rocky delicately entered their bedroom; and this is the moment of tears for me. He looked at his wife and said: "It's all I know, if I can't fight what else can I do?" He continued to look at Adrian and said, "You asking me to stop fighting is like me asking you to stop being a woman." Wow! For me, this is one of the greatest expressions of harmonious passion; the internalized identity he expressed pierced me and touched passion in me.

With this thought in mind, being in relationship with others who are in touch with their passion can feel more like a relative relationship than people who share your DNA. There is a recognizable and undeniable connection that brings people of healthy passion together. The object of passion does not have to be the same. The connection is about passion in general. There is a saying: "real recognizes real, and game recognizes game." I add: passion recognizes passion.

Take these examples into account; and do not simply view these as movies. These kinds of interactions and experiences happen every day, in the lives of passionate people. The content might vary from person-to-person, and from relationship-to-relationship; but do know that these are not just made-up movie issues. These are real-life, human issues. I hope you can now see how complex variables can become, as you continue to solidify your understanding of passion. This is why I have taken the time to consider many sides of this topic; I want to be sure you have good, sound information; and that you begin to think about passion differently.

While some actions in these examples seemed very selfish, extreme, and obsessive; in each film these men represent a larger population of people who deal with similar concerns. Perhaps you are a part of the larger population who can attest to such challenges, or you know of someone who can attest. My hope is that you will apply this knowledge going forward. I want you to truly understand what drives you, and follow hard after it.

Throughout this writing I have reverberated the idea that passion is a powerful force. Whether passion is harmonious or obsessive, passion drives and is unstopped. Passion must have liberty to do its thing. It is a quality that will not be denied if it is harmonious. However, if you remember the quality of obsessive passion, individuals are less likely to move on a passion if the outcome of performance does not lead to what individuals consider as successful. That is, individuals are more likely to engage in performance-avoidance in the face of an outcome that is predicted to be negative.

I am sure you are now reflecting on moments in your life when you experienced passion unstopped, regardless of what stood in your way or who might have tried to hold you back and discourage you. You would not and could not deny passion within. Have you ever started speaking with someone about something you are passionate toward? What do you remember about the interchange? Let me tell you about a story that is very recent as yesterday. I routinely set a timer for each therapy session, so that I can know when to begin to wind down, and allow five minutes to transition and end sessions. Yesterday was an unusual day. I was with my last client of the day. Ironically, we were discussing passion. After a while, I noticed it had become dark outside. By the time we *should* have been leaving, it would have been daylight still. I took a quick moment's glance at the clock, and realized we had gone over time. We should have already ended the session and left the building by now. Undoubtedly, I did not set the alarm. We both laughed when I told the client, we just experienced a real live example of what passion can and will do.

Safeguard Your Passion

Even with the purest of intention in mind, your harmonious passion could become an obsessive passion for you. With this thought in front of you, make a notation; you are responsible for safeguarding your passion! Early on I mentioned balance, boundaries, and self-care. The following are some ways to consider whether or not you are safeguarding your passion, and what you can begin to do if you are not:

- **Practice mindfulness**. The state of being conscious or aware is what mindfulness is all about. Not only mindfulness specific to self-awareness, but also other-awareness and situational-awareness. Included in mindfulness is being aware of thoughts that come up for you, whether or not you will allow thoughts to linger, and if so; why you will allow thoughts to linger. Finally, mindfulness is considering how you intend to process thoughts that you allow to linger.

    This means you will not be in your emotions, but in your head. You will

106

intentionally explore and address thoughts that require your attention. Only you can determine this. One way to determine what thoughts are worthy of exploration and addressing, is to weigh how heavy thoughts are in your mind. If certain thoughts won't go away, you might have unfinished business in that area. After exploring, you realize thoughts are not worthy of addressing; discard them and move on. If moving on from certain thoughts become challenging; clearly there is either something there that needs more of your attention; or you can benefit from therapeutic or self-help tools to learn how to deal with thought-stopping and neurotically replaying information, that swirls around in your head.

Also, it is important to take yourself through this mindfulness process, not only because achieving mindfulness is what this process is about; but because you gain more insight regarding how you are wired in your thought processes. You can gain more insight when you engage in metacognition, which is awareness and understanding of your thought processes. Metacognition is not just about your thoughts, but intelligently knowing your thoughts and thought processes.

Additionally, when engaging in metacognition, you can think about your thoughts rather than being carried away by your thoughts. With metacognition, you are not only thinking; you are also observing how you are thinking. This higher level of thinking can be mastered, and you can become better at managing what you will allow to linger in your mind and what you will let go. What happens next is the ability to be able to manage emotions more effectively. Ultimately you can make better life choices and interact with yourself, others, and the world in a healthier manner.

What does all this have to do with passion, you ask? When you are mindful, and when you critically examine thoughts to determine what will be allowed and what will be disallowed; you are able to enjoy healthy emotions. Even if you are in a bad state emotionally, you are more aware and can practice effective coping and emotion intelligence because your mind is healthy. Ultimately you can make good life decisions. All these together provide a platform and freedom for you to be in tune with your passion.

- **Be a forever learner.** As a practitioner, I am required to be a forever learner. Every two years my professional licenses are up for renewal. Before I can renew, I must have completed a certain amount of continuing education units (CEUs) for each state in which I hold a license.

  Although this is a requirement that is regulated by my licensing board; as a personal commitment to myself, I would want to be sure I am abreast of what is new and needful for me to know. I would want to keep myself adequately skilled and fine-tune what is necessary to practice effectively; this is my personal conviction. So be a forever learner. Stay innovative in your thought processes, cultivate emotional intelligence, and stay in-the-know regarding what is going on with you passionately.

- **Connect with people of healthy passions.** Along with mindfulness, and being a forever learner, you will do well to remain connected to people of passion. It does not matter what others are passionate about, just as long as their passions are healthy.

Take my word, you will need these connections. I told you the word for passion comes from the Latin word *passio*, which means to suffer. This is not in reference to suffering as a bad thing. But it is a thing; it is a part of passion because passion is relentless. As a person of passion, you will be misunderstood. You will spend days, nights, and seasons feeling very alone. This is why I encourage you to keep a contact list of healthy, passionate people accessible to you. The AA community has sponsors, so grab yourself a passion sponsor.

- **Foster healthy physical habits**. Healthy habits overall are recommended. Maintain a balanced life of good nutrition. Also, monitor your sensory intake. Be careful of what your eyes watch, your ears hear, your nose smells, your hands handle, and what your mouth tastes. This might sound like an extreme statement, but senses matter. If you know a particular show or series will distract you and hinder your ability to perceive accurately; make adjustments. Some shows are riddled with drama and can ultimately impact your thought life. This is true for what you eat, especially items that can cause moodiness. So, guard all of your senses carefully.

Journal writing to mind-dump and detox negative thoughts and emotions, can prove helpful. Foster good sleep hygiene. Remain aware when you are going down a path of creating unhealthy routines. Work hard to not become stuck in a rut: at work, home, in your romantic relationships, in your friendships, and in your relationship with yourself. Yes, I said your relationship with yourself. If you have not thought about you being in a relationship with yourself, allow me to share. A relationship with yourself includes your self-talk, your choice of entertainment, people you embrace and share your personal and valuable information with, and how you treat yourself in your decision-making, just to name a few.

- **Laugh often.** A good belly laugh on a regular basis is good for you. Feel good chemicals are released when you laugh. I consider myself to be a bit of a goofball and can laugh easily, at just about anything. I say this unapologetically because I know my life is so much better because I don't take everything so seriously.

Try this, schedule times to periodically watch a cartoon or comedy, not something that could ultimately have a negative impact on your mind, emotions, and mood. Try comedy that leaves you with a good feeling that you have done something good for you and you now have your life's well, filled with goodness. Recently, while preparing to get to the office; I passed by the television with a bowl of cereal in my hand. As I was eating, I stopped to glance at Tom and Jerry cartoon on the television. Before I knew it, I was laughing out loud. For a brief moment, I remembered what it was like as a kid. I am sure, in some way; taking this time to get in touch with my inner child, made a difference and added an extra boost of positive energy to my day.

You too have good vibes and energy to share and spread along the way as you are driving, or in the grocery store; or kicking it with your friends, having family time with your partner, children, or whomever. You are good within and without.

- **Share your ideas with others.** This is different from connecting with people of healthy passions. There are people who are lost and struggling with which direction to take. As you become more aware and proficient in your passion-filled life, share with someone else. You might be surprised about the humbling effect this can have on you, and you can remain energized with your never-ending story about passion.

"Die to everything of yesterday so that your mind is always fresh, always young, innocent, full of vigor and passion."

Jiddu Krishnamurti

CHAPTER V

THE NEVER-
ENDING STORY

Nowadays passion is discussed in many ways. Some people talk about passion in terms of their purpose, others speak of passion in terms of their skills or talents. There are also some who identify their inspirations as their passion. Regardless, passion is a never-ending story. For sure, no one is passionate about just one thing, or one person. Just recently, I was in my feelings. I was missing my children and thinking of many memories we created throughout the years.

As I was in deep thought and emotions, I realized there is no place on earth where I really feel at home. The only time I remember feeling a sense of home was as a child. The good thing about this is I can live just about anywhere and adjust; I claim no affinity to any one place in particular. While still in my thoughts and emotions, I experienced an epiphany. A moment of enlightenment hit me, I proceeded to text the following message to my children:

> Whenever I am with the two of you; it does not matter where we are, it feels like home. You are the best part of me.

When I'm with my children, it feels like home because of who they are, not because of where we are. My children are the object of my expressed passion; but not only my children, I have many more passions.

I'll share my first experience of identification with passion. After completion of my bachelor's degree, my next goal was to go on to graduate school. I received my bachelor's degree in the area of business, organizational management. It only made since that I would continue on the business track and pursue my MBA. I found the university I wanted to attend and applied to Holy Names University. My first night in class was an eye-opener. Nothing about what I heard coming from the professor was exciting to me. Sitting in class that night helped me to see that I was not going to enjoy this journey, should I continue.

My focus was not engaged, sort of felt like being in a loveless relationship. The problem for me was, I had no idea of which direction to take next. I went home very discouraged and I felt utterly lost and empty. My children and spouse were in their usual mood and engagement with me, but I was disconnected and inattentive. Not in a dismissive way that was noticeable. I was dealing with what my next step would be and I had no clue. Once the environment was quiet, I sat in the middle of my bed and stared at the wall. While staring, my gazed turned to my bookcase that was arranged diagonally against the wall.

There were many books I had gathered over the course of my studies, including books from the time I pursued an associate degree. Among my collection were a few books from undergraduate studies at Patten

University, where I earned my bachelor's degree. In that program of study, the requirement was to take one course on religion, since the college was a bible-based institution. I chose a class on Christian counseling. The instructor was amazing and I thoroughly enjoyed the class. As I stared at my collection of books, three books by the same author (Larry Crabb) stared back at me.

While scanning my books, I decided I would read. I chose to read: The Safest Place on Earth: Where People Connect and Are Forever Changed. I can still remember as if it were just yesterday. I read the entire book sitting in the middle of my bed. Here is where passion comes in. Something was ignited in my spirit and in my heart; I could not shake it. I felt engaged again. All of my confusion and disillusionment disappeared. As I prepared for bed, I knew that I had to reach out to Holy Names to determine what programs were available for counseling. Not many days later, I received a brochure and an application. I applied and was accepted. I began classes the following year, in the spring semester.

Do you remember what I wrote earlier, about knowing I would not enjoy the MBA program? Here was my response to the counseling psychology master's program: I sat with my eyes glued to the professor. I hung on every word and got lost in time. Just as I could not see myself in the MBA program, I could not see myself anywhere except the counseling psychology program. By the time I graduated, two years and some months felt like nothing.

This was my first experience with passion. Another experience builds onward as I pursued licensure as a therapist. It took another two years and some months, but time was not a factor. I gladly did what was necessary because I was passionate. Working for non-profits organizations was fun and taught me a lot; but after a few years something was missing. I began to feel the same emptiness I felt when I was in the first night of class, for the MBA program.

I took as much knowledge, information, and experience from my years of working for others; and I began to think of myself in terms of private practice. Five years had passed, from the first time I thought to establish my private practice. Still, no private practice. I relocated from California to Texas, and thought I would begin by working for a reputable company that paid lots of money for my credentials and skills; then I could begin to execute my plan.

Real soon, necessity of funds became my greatest focus. I began to wonder and ask; Crystal, what in all of creation are you doing? I felt like I was out here floundering. I found myself in a new state, with my degree and experience, and difficulty securing employment. Then I remembered something I heard in my heart and mind, during my relocation process from California. As I cleaned my garage and packed boxes; I heard this: you will never work for anyone again. Now of course when money got low, I rebuked that voice and desperately sought work.

The never-ending story gets better. My employment hunt did not go well, and this is when doubt began to creep in. I started to wonder why I was not being accepted for positions I was well qualified for. At this point I was licensed in two states, I thought to myself: this has to count for something. It was little scary I must admit. The only thing left to do was to remember the voice telling me I would never work for anyone again. You see, funds were running low and I had to do something to keep from feeling like an utter and complete failure.

What did I do next you ask? I decided to search for office space. Yes; I know my money was running low, and I decided to gamble with a possibility of securing office space; sounds insane, right? Let me add, I had not begun any kind of marketing to secure patients. I was in network with only a couple of insurance companies as a provider and no one called to schedule. By this time, I only had risks to take and nothing to lose.

So, I paid for the deposit and first months rent for office space, and then flew out to California for a mini vacation. Sounds insane again? Believe me when I say, nothing about my plans sounded like common sense. But this is good news. Passion does not seem to make sense at times. I had become so tired that I did not consider the facts: I had no job, my funds were depleting quickly, and I had no patients scheduled. To add insult to injury; I decided to spend what little money I had left on office space, for which I had no furniture. Then I took a trip. How about that?

Yes, I was doing all this with many deficiencies. But as I stated earlier, I had nothing to lose. Doing something felt a lot better than doing nothing. I took a chance and eventually everything turned out just fine. In time, I got started on what I was passionate about all along, my private practice. Before I could do so, I had to deal with having my back completely against the wall. I did not think about being afraid of failure. I was all out there at this point.

I am sure you can hardly wait to hear what happened in the interim. The first day of my vacation in California, my cell phone began ringing and did not stop until I had approximately seven clients scheduled. This happened in a span of a couple of hours. I was blown away. I could hardly contain myself. My experience was told to everyone I knew near and far, basically anyone who would listen. Then it hit me, Crystal; you have no office furniture. Was I a little shaken? Yes, I was. I did not allow myself to keep focus on what I did not have. At this point I knew I'd figure something out. My courage was returning because my passion was back in the driver's seat. Looking back on the leaps I took and how my faith did not fail me, I refused to think I was going to hit a brick wall. Even if I did, my confidence was way up; and I was not going to allow anything to discourage me.

When I arrived back to Texas, I had a few days before my very first patient would come to see me. When I say my beginning was humble, take my word. In my cute little office suite was one small table with a couple of magazines on top for decoration. This table sat in the middle of two dining room chairs. Quality chairs, but certainly not office chairs. I had a couple of pictures on the wall, and a tall standing lamp in the corner of the office. That's it! That was the extent of my office on opening day.

You might wonder what was going through my mind and what emotions I experienced. More than anything, I wondered if my first patient would return for a follow-up visit; and she did. In fact, she returned for many more. The following week I had a couple's session scheduled. You must know the two-chair setup was not going to work out. I was right back in a quandary. What was I going to do, I asked myself? I told my husband what my dilemma was, and he said let's go and take a ride. We rode around and came across a furniture store. There was one comfy two-seater couch that caught my eye, that was reasonably priced. I thought to myself, God heard my prayer and saw what I needed.

We purchased the couch and loaded it onto my husband's truck. While bringing in my couch into the office, the person across the hall from my suite donated a desk. He was moving out and had no need for it. There you have it, my office was finally coming together. When I tell this story, I often say I wish I had kept pictures because I never want to forget my humble beginnings and how far I have come. I have faith and I trust that God blessed me with passion and helped me, but I had to do my part.

Oh, I forgot to mention inspiration and passion to write and publish my first book, in 2007. This experience took a lot of courage because unknown authors really have to work hard to become known. I knew I had something to say to encourage and be of help to others, but I did not have an idea of success as writer in mind. I just knew I wanted to write, and I had an overflow of information waiting to flow. My goal was to begin and reach as many people who would give an ear to what I have to say. Today as I write this is book, number five; I still have more to say. Moreover, I went beyond what I originally planned and expected as an author. My third book was accepted by Barnes and Noble and made it to their shelf.

In 2017 I began filming clips of topic discussions I have addressed over the years as a therapist. By 2018 an inspiration hit me to produce a talk show. While researching how to get started, I ran across current talk shows and offers to become a part of the audience. I applied to a few and received tickets to The Wendy Williams Show. I was excited to have an opportunity to be up close and personal, and have firsthand knowledge of what really goes on behind the scenes.

After looking for reasonably priced tickets and hotels in such a short time; I was able to plan my travel and ultimately become a part of a wonderful experience, and to see New York for the very first time. When I returned home and gathered my thoughts, I remembered thinking; gee, developing and hosting a talk show sure is a lot of work. But the desire was still there. I thought about it more and more, and then began to script out how I wanted my show to be produced.

Did I have questions about how things would work out? Yes, I did. Did I wonder if I was making the right move or just going on emotions? Yes, I absolutely did wonder. Nevertheless, the mindset I held helped me to distinguish the difference between emotions and passions. I had to remind myself that emotions are ever shifting and changing. Passion will not let me sleep (in a good way, not neurotically like obsessive passion). When I am passionate about something; I can try to ignore it, substitute it, and downplay it, but it is always there. If I try to distract myself with other things; passion waves at me as from afar, like a close friend who has been missing me. Passion reminds me that I can either engage or be miserable. Now I realize that I can ignore passion and never get to what I am passionate about; however, if I do; my life will be dreary, and my jovial and bubbly spirit would cease.

With all the understanding and experience I have related to passion, stuck moments still come. Most recently, before working on episode 2 of my talk show, there was no spark to write, create, or do anything that felt like passion for me. I took that time to engage more in fun and relaxing activities, and give extra attention to healthcare. At first, I felt like something was missing. Perhaps I felt this way because for a while my passions consistently flowed. Before long, I realized I was on a much-needed break; and now I can accept this as a part of the process.

We all have a story, and it connects to many other stories we have to tell. What is your story? Give it some thought. As I shared earlier; the more self-aware you are, the more you will pinpoint passion moments. Don't become so busy and entangled in the busyness of life that you miss what you are truly passionate about. If you are in a phase of life and you are feeling humdrum, you might be disconnected from passion, passion that drives your life. Know this, not a person or thing can replace passion that you must do something with. Passion is very personal. You can operate in your passion with others; but others cannot fulfill or replace what you are uniquely, and individually driven to do. I reiterate, passion is personal!

It only takes one,
So why not you.
Sure, others can do it,
But so can you.
The only thing that's in your way,
Is your mindset: the doubtful words you choose to say.
There's a battle for your passion, a fight;
At times you think, something is just not right.
You feel lost, out of sorts and don't know what to do,
It's a part of the process, it's not something new.
You see, anything worth experiencing is worth
going through the challenges and the doubts.
Trust me; pretty soon, you will figure things out.
Buckle up, hold on tight, and stay the course;
What you gain will be worth the work.
Calm down and relax, no need to worry,
Passion is not a one-time experience,
it's a never-ending story.

While passion is a never-ending story, everyone's story is different; and many factors and variables interplay that speak to individuals' process. I shared with you my story as an adult; now I will share with you concepts I conclude as important when I ponder my life leading to adulthood. These concepts are: *era, exhortation, exposure, and experience.* You too will do well to consider these concepts, as you understand how they have shaped your understanding and experience of passion. If you are more likely to doubt yourself because you are not as advanced as you think you should be, especially when you compare yourself to others; allow these concepts to shed light on your thoughts.

Era. Factors such as era, generation, and society played a major role in my perceptions, perspectives, and emotions. For a long time; such factors also impacted the way I relate to myself, others, and the world. Even till today; I continue working diligently at refraining from old thinking and behaviors, in order to open my mind to new information and live passionately.

To my point, do I remember specifically being spoken to about passion? No, I cannot say I was; in fact, I do not recall the word "passion" being used at all. Looking back, were there behaviors that represented passion, although I was not aware that I was in the midst of passion, being expressed; absolutely! Can I say for sure that I knew what was harmonious passion or what was obsessive passion? I absolutely cannot say this. Here is my dilemma: could it be that my lack of understanding of passion was not only about era; but also due to a lack of resources and ignorance.

Not ignorance in a derogatory manner, but ignorance based on a lack of knowledge. These are some things to consider, how about you do the same?

Being born in the late sixties; no doubt there was not as much information about passion as we know today. But I do believe others of my era, in other regions of the world, were privy to what I did not experience. Do I get down on myself for what I did not know, no way! As you consider any limitations of your era, I also do not want you to get down on yourself. I stated in my book on communication: you know what you know, until you know more; and you are where you are until you arrive at the place where you are headed. Along with era, I realize exhortation as a factor that informs how I make sense of my experience with passion, or lack thereof.

Exhortation. Of course, if I cannot recall being cognizant of the meaning of passion, chances are I did not experience the concept of exhortation. This does not mean I was not exhorted. Perhaps my lack of understanding elements of passion, resulted in me missing times of exhortation. As I am reflecting now, I do remember my mother regularly reminding me of how smart I was at age two or three.

My mom told me that I was able to recite the entire preamble to the constitution. She would have me to recite it to others. Academically, I never struggled and the only class I failed was physical education. Only because I was defiant and refused to change into my physical education uniform, until it was time for me to graduate; then I found a new respect for my physical education uniform. Although I received praise for my academic accomplishments; does this mean praise led to passion, did my passion for learning promote praise, or both? Whichever is true, exhortation matters in relation to passion.

Regardless of the age or time in life when exhortation begins; you can begin awareness and experience of passion. When you are strongly urged and encouraged by others as they notice or observe your passion, this can make a difference. Not only are era and exhortation factors that inform understanding and experience of passion, exposure is an important factor as well.

Exposure. You will not expand if you are not exposed. Exposure includes a repetitious engagement to build principles and understanding of passion. Speaking about passion and being in the midst of people who model passion in their lives can be helpful, but exposure has to ultimately lead to practice for you.

The more you are able to understand what passion is, the more likely you can recognize passion when you interface with people, things, and activities that draw on your harmonious passion. But what if you were not exposed to passion? This could be why you doubt at times, why you might feel somber and not in tune with your truest self. Even if you are just beginning now, no worries. It is never too late to become exposed to passion and live a fully passionate life. Remember, this information is designed to help you understand reasons why you might be stuck; and aid you as you embrace passion going forward. Finally, in addition to era, exhortation, and exposure; experience matters.

Experience. At this point, you will do well to truly introspect. Although you might have been restricted by your era, generation, region, or family; I am sure you can locate passion in some moments and areas of your life. Passion might have been underdeveloped, but it was there.

As you reflect, maybe your experience was not breathtaking and perhaps you do not recall feelings of being wowed; but for sure there was something passionate if you take the time to rediscover it. As a child, pretending to bake mud pies and be a school teacher was something I recall doing in my spare time.

Today, I still enjoy teaching and cooking. Hobbies were few for me; but what I enjoyed doing, I really enjoyed. Whenever I got the time be alone with myself, I enjoyed it as well. Being alone was restorative solitude for me. I would play with my dolls and pretend to be a mommy; and enjoy my own little world I created.

For the most part, I have followed through with activities I engaged in as a child. I became a mommy, spouse, and although I have never been a school teacher in particular; everything about what I do today in my life involves teaching. How about you? Stop here and take a moment to think about it. Go to the end of this book, and in the notes section; write down your thoughts. Also, if you do not already do so; consider the following to begin building your repertoire of experiences that could foster a sense of passion for you:

Travel. Travel can be tailored to whatever fits your style; but do travel. The older I become, the less inclined I am to travel by plane. I will if necessary; but I am not as much of a fan of planes as I once was.

I am definitely a fan of road trips. Even if road trips are for a number of days, I enjoy the opportunity to stop and lodge wherever I am, and enjoy where I am on the way to where I am headed. If you are a traveler by car you resonate with the excitement radiating from these pages as I write. In fact, traveling by car affords more of an opportunity to stop when I desire; such opportunities are not afforded if you travel by bus or train. However, you are able to see more on a bus or train, versus a plane. It's your choice, so choose!

There is not a right or wrong way of relating to this idea. Some people do not enjoy the length of time it takes to travel by car; take a bus, or travel by train. Some people like to get to their destination as quickly as possible. Your mode of travel does not matter; just be sure to get outside of your comfort zone and surround yourself with other visions of the world.

Travel to other countries if you are really determined and brave. If you are not so brave, travel to another state. Some states are closely connected. So much so; that you can drive an hour from one state; and end up in another state. If you are not ready to travel between states and countries; try traveling to another city in your current state and maybe you can branch out later. If the idea of traveling to another city is not appealing to you, at least leave your neighborhood and familiar surrounding areas.

You will be hard-pressed to grow, develop, enhance your knowledge, and get the most out of passion until you explore and learn new information. Exploration and exposure add to your understanding, even if you do not like what you have come to understand. There is a lesson in every experience if you are ripe to absorb.

Art. Culinary is a style of art that I am particularly fond of. What is yours? Getting in touch with your artistic side can spark creativity. The part of your brain that is responsible for creativity is activated when you engage in any kind of art. Who knows what you will discover once you get started? Mix it up. If you are into free-form art, go for it. Some people get lost in creativity of fine arts, graphic arts, and the like. Listen, if the only art you are interested in is painting by numbers, painting with a twist, or coloring in a jumbo coloring book; whatever it is, just do it! I recently learned about the following paint activities in various states: trap bounce and paint, trap-n-paint, and paint and chill. See what you can come up with.

Diversity. We are living in times of pervasive, cultural diversity. Nowadays, many places are considered melting pots, making it easier to experience cultural diversity from wherever you are. I want you to also consider diversity in other forms such as age, gender, and socioeconomics. Don't limit yourself. For sure you live near or work with someone who is not a part of your culture, age, and socioeconomic status. Turn those relationships into opportunities to learn something new. Some people pay money to study diversity courses; but you can get your diversity education for free. Also, take advantage of social media. There are many ways to connect with groups of all kinds. There are options of face-to-face group involvement or virtual groups.

Music. Regardless of the genre of music you prefer, try mixing it up a bit. Certain music might be what suits your style and personality; but you will be surprised at how your brain can be impacted by introducing something different. Such a change and introduction of new information through music could possibly create new pathways in your brain.

According to the term neuroplasticity, your brain is able to form and reorganize synaptic connections when introducing a new learning experience to your brain. Scientists have studied and report that the brain's neural pathways can be trained and rewired. This process can add to regulation of emotions, thoughts, and reactions. These pathways are called highways in the brain that can take you to experiences of compassion, gratitude, and decreased anxiety and other negative emotions.

Unfortunately, the opposite or negative experience is possible as well. By this I mean; if you are not living a passion filled life, you can become emotionally upset over a period of time. The more you train yourself to doubt and convince yourself that you are not good enough; you actually change the brain. You create new pathways. Just as doing positive things with your brain can lead to improved emotions and functioning; the more you train yourself toward negativistic thinking; your emotions and mood are more likely to become depressed and anxious.

As you implement new experiences in your life, you will also experience a noticeable difference in how you think. Your language and conversation will change because you have been exposed to so much more. Being enlightened by insight can make a world of a difference. Depositing these principles in your life is like depositing money into the bank; and the yielded interest is phenomenal. As applied, various encounters can be like sperm to your egg; before you know it, conception takes place. You become pregnant with more and more passionate experiences.

*"If a founder has passion and innovation,
he needs to be supported…"*

Ratan Tata

Chapter VI

PAY IT FORWARD

The term "pay it forward" is described as responding to an act of kindness toward you by being kind to someone else. I have shared pertinent information with you regarding passion. For some, this is your first time reading about passion in this context; for others this is a refresher of information. Whichever is the case for you, pay it forward.

Take some time to share with someone what you now know. This will not be a difficult task for you if you are passionate about disseminating information to others, if you like sharing with others something new you have discovered, and if you enjoy teaching and modeling new concepts. Are you familiar with the movie, "Pay It Forward?"

This movie is about showing good will toward others. The teacher in this film challenged students to do something that changes the world. What happened in this movie not only resulted in a broad impact in the movie, but today we still use the term of paying it forward. The idea has taken hold of individuals who gain a sense of appreciation for good deeds shown to them, and want others to experience the same good feeling.

Paying it forward is not only about sharing your experiences regarding passion, but also about who you are authentically and healthily related to passion. If paying it forward will be a genuine experience for you and for those who receive from your passionate life; you will need to cultivate a life that shows and glows. This book is about unrestrained passion. I want you to have good ideas and tools for your journey of a passion filled life. The following are some examples of areas of your life and activities to explore, in order to determine how equipped and prepared you are, to effectively experience passion.

Home. How healthy are you in your home life? Are your relationships fulfilling and conducive to the best you? If your homelife is stressful, and unsatisfying, this can interfere with your overall satisfaction. Even when you are in touch with your passions, an unhealthy homelife can create dissatisfaction in things you would otherwise enjoy. While you are not responsible for the way others treat or respond to you; your responsibility is how you respond to unfavorable relationships.

Are you able to stay in your sweet place mentally and emotionally if your spouse or romantic partner is unloving and unkind to you on a regular basis? What about if your children are being unruly and diffficult, can you remain focused on effective selfcare, and remain true to passions that fulfill you.

Extended family and in-law relatives can also prove challenging. How do you manage all these ties and interactions when they are over-the-top stressful? While no plan is fail-proof; I have heard this statement before and it resonates for me: "if you fail to plan, you plan to fail." Having a plan and not needing one, is far better than needing a plan and not having one. Stay equipped.

Work. Not everyone will find their job or career satisfying. Some people work in stressful jobs because of necessity. Not everyone can just quit a job when they are not satisfied. However, you do not have to allow a dissatisfying job to jeopardize your passion.

While working various jobs and in graduate school, I did not like some of the jobs; but I kept my focus on what I was working toward. Every opportunity I had, I pulled out my textbooks and I would read. I needed these reminders of what I was working toward. Whatever works for you, keep your vision in front view somehow. If your workplace is not what stimulates passion; surround yourself, as much as you can, with passionate activities you can engage in. Consider volunteering in a field you are passionate toward.

Volunteering. Surrounding yourself by people with like passions, in a volunteer role, can help when work is dissatisfying. There are many volunteer opportunities and you might find this as an exciting way to pay it forward, and a way to keep yourself passionately stimulated at the same time.

You might make it a little easier on yourself if you implement deductive reasoning; and identify things you know for certain you are not interested in. For example, if you are not interested in the heat; you know for sure that your volunteer direction will not be outdoor activities in the summer months, in Texas; or in the winter months in Chicago.

Literature. Engaging in current research can be a way to add to your well when things seem to be running a little dry. Of course, there are times when you might not know the direction to take. Self-awareness can help. If you are a person who is drawn to problem-solving and psychological thrillers; you probably will not spend a lot of time reading romance novels. When you know yourself, you have some inkling of what "your thing" is. Go with what you already know about yourself. Incorporate workshops and training events. Invest in insight-oriented therapy, or a life coach to help you figure things out.

Hobbies. What are some hobbies that you have not tried: hiking, fishing, sports, horseback riding, etc.? It is okay to do whatever you choose; but I challenge you to consider getting out of your comfort zone. You can learn even more about yourself as you stimulate your brain by introducing new information. As you are learning new skills, you are also learning more about what you like; and this learning can lead to passionate moments.

Leisure activities, relaxation, and exercise. Try doing some things alone intentionally, especially if this is a challenge for you. Why do I say this, you ask? While you can certainly learn about yourself and improve self-awareness in the presence of others; it is also important to be alone with you and your own assessment and evaluation of *YOU,* without influence and energy of others.

How do you generally relax? Are you open to trying different ways of relaxing? Whatever you choose, remember this; relaxation is whatever feels relaxing to you. Your approach might include doing something; or doing nothing at all. There is no right or wrong way to relax. If you feel relaxed, rejuvenated, and healthy; and your passion is not thwarted, go for it! And what about exercising? Especially if you are more likely to engage in only one form of exercise; try cycling, yoga, zumba, or any form of exercise you have not tried.

Meetup groups. Such groups can be a good support. Your style and needs matter. Most, if not all groups allow you to narrow your search criteria to suit or fit your specific needs and desires. If you have never tried this avenue of interaction, give it a test. Try out the process. Don't forget to get in touch with your explorative side and challenge yourself to be in a group setting with others who are different from you. This might prove to be an interesting learning experience that can spark passion.

Are you a person who likes to build and create things? Are you good with your hands? Are you a person more interested in relationships, social issues, and helping; such as being a person of human resources? Are you more of a numbers or scientific person? Are you more chilled and laid back, or are you daring and more open to trying new things? Are you spontaneous, or are you highly structured? Do you possess a strong affinity for animals? Are you more of the outdoorsy type, or more of a person who is considered a home bodied person? What types of environments do you tend to thrive and flourish in?

If you are you ready and willing to challenge yourself, to go against what you have become routinized in doing, and to create new learning pathways; the moment is now! Do you prefer being around a certain age group, or population of people? Is this something you are willing to change up a bit? Consider making small changes at first, just to test your comfort level. But remember, to understand yourself better and to learn if there are things you might be passionate toward; you will do well to stop doing the same thing over and over again. Especially if you are experiencing the same results that you do not like.

I trust that this reading has already sparked a fire in you to become passionate about sharing. For the person who demonstrates healthy passions, paying it forward is a joy. Healthy people are balanced, and they enjoy life and experiences. Remember, psychological and emotional well-being are components of a life that is harmoniously passionate. I have composed the following poem for your consideration and encouragement:

Pay It Forward

You have what someone wants and need,
You realize it and you are happy to extend the deed.
Upon reflecting, you recall the times you doubted,
You felt lost, distraught, at times
you screamed and shouted.
Answers you desired, resolutions you sought,
Tiring and painful was the fight you fought.
But one day someone came along,
Someone who spoke to your passion, and
your life was like a new song.
How could you deny it?
When your passion was revealed to
you, everything seemed to fit;

Then one day someone crossed your
path and immediately,
You could see, that what you had, someone needed it.
Without hesitation, and without delay,
You hastened to reach out, to extend your
hand and show someone the way.
It all began with a healthy passion to spread the word,
To impart hope of a passion-filled life, to
share your desire; and pay it forward!

Affirming yourself is a tool that can be very supportive as you live your life of passion. To affirm yourself means you are proclaiming, asserting, and declaring words of encouragement. I can assure you there will be times on your path to exercising your new understanding of passion, that you will be happy to have affirmations. Take a look at some I have shared with you; come up with some of your own.

AFFIRMATIONS

1. I am good enough for where I am in life and for what I am doing. If I am lacking certain skills, I am capable of learning and improving.

2. I and my limitations are not one in the same. My limitations do not define the essence of who

I am. My limitations do not prevent me from being good enough.

3. I am who I am until I evolve into what I will be.

4. I know what I know until I know more.

5. I am where I am until I arrive where I am headed.

6. I do my best, and I am careful not to allow others to raise a standard for me.

7. My mind is my most powerful weapon against negativity.

8. There are no failures, no losses, and no wasted time for me. Every experience is a valuable lesson.

9. Since I have to *live* my life, I refuse to allow others to plan it.

10. I will not succumb to comparison.

11. Having weaknesses and limitations means nothing other than being human.

12. Aiming at nothing or aiming at something; in either scenario a decision has been made, I will decide wisely.

13. I will not live my life hoping yesterday gets better.

14. I give grace to myself in preparation for giving grace to others.

15. I pledge to treat myself with the utmost respect, and refuse to embrace disrespect from any source.

16. If I keep my gaze backwards, I am subject to become depressed; if I keep my gaze fixed on the future of things beyond my control, I might become anxious. I will focus on my present moments and do the very best I can.

17. Very few things in life are guaranteed, change is one of those few things. I can protest change, or embrace change and experience peace.

18. The last time I engaged in approval seeking behavior was my last time.

19. Each day I will wash off the cares of life and adorn myself with possibilities of a new day's experiences.

20. Criticism can be a good thing or bad thing, depending on what I call it.

21. I cannot afford the costliness of a negative attitude.

22. I will not hold anything or anyone so closely, that I cannot let go if I have to, or if I choose to.

23. Losing myself in any situation is not an option, I am the one person I am depending on to be there for me.

24. I am practicing patience toward myself and toward others.

25. In disagreement with others, I am making perspective-taking a practice to prioritize.

26. A little understanding can go a long way.

27. I will learn to be mindful of my thoughts, for they impact my emotions, moods, and my actions.

28. I no longer see the sky as the limit.

29. Boundaries keep me and others safe. Boundaries keep dangerous things going from me to others, and from others to me.

30. If I stay focused, disciplined, structured, and realistic; I am bound to accomplish my goals.

31. I am too valuable to settle for less than my worth.

32. Sometimes I have to capture a vision for something before I actually experience it.

CHAPTER VII

SATISFACTION AND PASSION SURVEYS

Satisfaction Questionnaire

Self-report measure by Fetzer Institute

7-Strongly agree

6-Agree

5-Slightly agree

4-Neither agree nor disagree

3-Slightly disagree

2-Disagree

1-Strongly disagree

____In most ways, my life is close to my ideal.

____The conditions of my life are excellent.

____I am satisfied with my life.

____So far, I have gotten the important things I want in life.

____If I could live my life over, I would change almost nothing.

SATISFACTION SURVEY
Scoring

31-35………. Extremely satisfied

26-30………. Satisfied

21-25………. Slightly satisfied

20……………. Neutral

15-19………. Slightly dissatisfied

10-14………. Dissatisfied

5-9……………Extremely dissatisfied

Passion Survey

---

1. Imagine spending a morning at each of these tasks. Which would make you feel most satisfied?

   - Brainstorming new ideas with a group of creative thinkers.

   - Attending a talk by an inspirational leader in your field.

   - Helping a vulnerable client find a solution to a long-term problem.

   - Taking part in boundary-breaking, team-building exercises.

2. If you went back to learning, which course would you be most attracted to?

   - An MBA, MSc or PhD- an intellectual challenge and an upgrade for your current qualifications.

- Personal growth- NLP, the Hoffman Process, or anything aimed at communication and relationships.
- Creative- writing, art, design, performance, photography or acting.
- Caring- social work, counseling, nursing, or teaching.

3. When looking back on your life, what will you hope to see that you have done?
   - Lasting and meaningful relationships with friends, colleagues and family.
   - That you fully explored and developed your creative talents.
   - That you went the extra mile to make a difference for others.
   - That you never stopped learning and growing as a person.

4. If you overheard colleagues gossiping about you, which comment would upset you most?
   - 'She has no imagination.'
   - 'She is not as popular as she thinks.'
   - 'She is a dinosaur stuck in the past.'
   - She is only out for number one.'

5. What traits do you find the most difficult in other people?
   - Self-centeredness and narcissism.
   - A closed mind and unwillingness to embrace new ideas.
   - Rigidity and an unquestioning following of rules.
   - Unkindness and lack of empathy.

6. What do you find the most rewarding about your work?
   - I am learning and growing as a person all the time.
   - It is an outlet for my creativity.
   - It has been a source of some of my closest friendships.
   - I feel as if I am making a difference to people who need help.

7. What would make you take a political candidate seriously?
   - Support for the arts, increasing participation locally or nationally.
   - Resources for housing, education and healthcare for the disadvantaged.
   - Lower university tuition fees and investment in research.

- Tax breaks and benefits to support family life and flexible working.

8. If a child asked you what is important in life, you would reply…
   - Be useful and kind.
   - Never take loved ones for granted.
   - Keep an open mind, keep learning.
   - Enjoy the beauty of our world.

9. You have inherited a large amount of money. Where are you most likely to donate it?
   - To setting up a local charity to provide low-cost counseling.
   - To helping develop an innovate technique to introduce education to repeat offenders.
   - To a local theatre, gallery, or cinema, to prevent it from closing down.

10. Which of the following phrases most closely matches your personal mission statement?
    - Build meaningful relationships with others.
    - Reach your full potential.
    - Celebrate the beauty of life.
    - Spread kindness and compassion.

You may find this (What is your true passion?) electronic survey at psychologies.co.uk.

My Survey Results

I participated in the survey. I could not have put the words more accurately. There is nothing in my results that is off as related to my passion. The following information below describes my results:

"You believe in going the extra mile—or even 26.2 miles for a charity marathon—to make the world a better place. It may be something that has always been important to you, or something that has grown in recent years, but you are convinced that the power of kindness can improve relationships and life in general, both locally and globally. You may already have found yourself drawn to working in a caring profession, such as social services, nursing or counseling. But your values can also be expressed in other professions. Living compassionately often goes hand-in-hand with a well-developed sense of empathy, and you may find it easy to step into another person's shoes. This can be expressed in many aspects of the corporate world, in jobs that rely on building trust and good relationships with clients. If your job is at odds with this core value, seek to nurture it outside the office, perhaps in voluntary work."

Passion Survey #2

**Questions for discovering what inspires
passion in your life—and what defeats it.**

---

1) Living passionately includes knowledge, awareness, and celebration of your pleasures in life, even the simplest pleasures. Prepare a list of things that are pleasurable for you. In doing so, you can figure out patterns of pleasure that lead to passion awareness.

_____

_____

_____

_____

_____

_____

_____

2) What activity involvements are you most likely to become excited about? Do you anticipate opportunities to engage in such activities? List them here.

_____

_____

_____

_____

_____

_____

_____

3) Scan the archives of your mind. As you scan, what do you notice that is jaw-dropping and eye-popping? What are some things that include "wowing" factors?

_____

_____

_____

_____

_____

_____

_____

4) When passionate about something, you follow hard after it, it comes up in conversations regularly, you journal about it, and study to gain more awareness of it. Name some of these things in your life.

_____

_____

_____

_____

_____

_____

_____

5) In this reading, you have learned about flow and passion. Flow involves commitment, energy, creativity, excitement, and endurance. As you reflect on your past and current experiences, jot down some experiences that fit the idea of passionate flow.

_____

_____

_____

_____

_____

_____

_____

6) You might be capable and skilled at recognizing what is trying to manifest in your life while in conversations with others, in your workplace, and in relationships and general interactions throughout your life's journey. At this very moment, what do think is trying to surface that might point to passion for you?

_____

_____

_____

_____

_____

_____

_____

7) A healthy life involves growth, development, and change. Have you been pondering changes you would like to implement? What are they?

_____

_____

_____

_____

_____

_____

_____

8) What do you like mostly about yourself? Why?

_____

_____

_____

_____

_____

_____

_____

9) If you could be a superhero which would you be? Why?

_____

_____

_____

_____

_____

_____

_____

10) Name movies that touch you deeply and you do not mind them repeatedly.

_____

_____

_____

_____

_____

_____

_____

11) What shows up as a strong desire in your life on a regular basis?

_____

_____

_____

_____

_____

_____

_____

12) Bring your awareness to one or more persons you admire. How do they inspire you?

_____

_____

_____

_____

_____

_____

_____

13) Who currently serves or has served as a mentor for you? Imagine this person is now assigned to advise you and guide you regarding direction to your passionate life. How is this mentor advising you? What is s/he speaking and modeling for you?

_____

_____

_____

_____

_____

_____

_____

14) Have you ever thrown caution to the wind and lived boldly? Describe boldness in your life today.

_____

_____

_____

_____

_____

_____

_____

15) Are you satisfied in your career/job? What are some positive changes that you can make in this area of your life?

_____

_____

_____

_____

_____

_____

_____

16) I identified the movie, Rocky, as a movie with compelling scenes of courage and tenacity. Name movie scenes that stand out for you. Scenes that touch you passionately. Scenes such as enduring love, words of affirmation, forgiveness, acts of services, advocates for justice, inspirational speaking, etc.

_____

_____

_____

_____

_____

_____

_____

17) Can you recall an offense or something that resulted in righteous indignation for you, something that spurred you on or motivated you to respond? This could be powerful insight that leads to identification of passion for you.

_____

_____

_____

_____

_____

_____

_____

18) When you watch the news or scroll through social media, what do you see and hear that perturbs you and unnerves you?

_____

_____

_____

_____

_____

_____

_____

19) You are a healthy human being if you are striving and thriving. The healthier you are in all areas of your life, the more you develop properly; and the more likely you are to experience a strong sense of self that connects you uniquely with your passion. When you are in your elements of passion, you invest all of YOU into the object of your passion. Name some of your healthy qualities that signify you are on the path to living a passionate life.

_____

_____

_____

_____

_____

_____

_____

20) Create a list of things you would like to accomplish before you die. Learn how to sew, fly a plane, surf, get a tattoo, write a book, reconcile a relationship, etc.

_____

_____

_____

_____

_____

_____

_____

21) Do you like yourself? Why?

_____

_____

_____

_____

_____

_____

_____

22) If you are faced with an opportunity to create signs that represent various directions in life one could take, what would your signs have written on them?

_____

_____

_____

_____

_____

_____

_____

23) William Shakespeare said: "The eyes are the window to your soul." When you look into the mirror while washing your face, brushing your teeth, combing your hair, applying your makeup, etc.; what do your eyes show you?

_____

_____

_____

_____

_____

_____

_____

24) Jot down your dreams. If dreams lead to enlightenment, what do your dreams reveal about you?

_____

_____

_____

_____

_____

_____

_____

25) What decision could you make today that your future self would thank you for?

_____

_____

_____

_____

_____

_____

_____

26) You are scrolling through screen savers to have a passion-inspiring message in front of you regularly, what is the screensaver message of your choice?

_____

_____

_____

_____

_____

_____

_____

27) Your past self is speaking to your current and future self; describe the conversation. What are the praises? What are the regrets?

_____

_____

_____

_____

_____

_____

_____

WHAT DEFEATS PASSION

- Have you allowed networking opportunities and invites pass you by that could have been leads to passion awareness for you? Discuss below.

  _____

  _____

  _____

  _____

  _____

  _____

- Do you allow bloodsucking parasites to suck the life out of your vitality? Some examples would be countless hours of mindlessly watching television, saying yes to requests to avoid feeling guilty for saying no, attending engagements when you are limited on time, overindulging in social media activities, talking endlessly with individuals about conversations that are meaningless and result in nothing, etc. Make a list of such things that are specific for you.

_____

_____

_____

_____

_____

_____

- Two types of boredom exist. One type is existential which consists of marital or other committed relationship or your career. Situational boredom consists of temporary circumstances such as standing in long lines at the DMV or sitting in traffic. What aspects of your life are you bored with?

_____

_____

_____

_____

_____

_____

- Thoughts and beliefs can drain you just as bloodsucking activities drain you. A list of thoughts include but are not limited to self-talk such as: I am not good enough, I am not smart, I will always be single and alone, I will always be broke, my life is not exciting, I can't do anything right, no one likes me, I will never amount to anything. Identify thoughts you rehearse, that are draining and limiting you.

_____

_____

_____

_____

_____

_____

- Action is required to deal with a boring life. Exploration is the way to understanding and insight, that leads to action in order to address a boring, lackluster life. As you reflect and explore your life, what comes up for you that is deep within and wants to express itself passionately?

_____

_____

_____

_____

_____

_____

- Are you a procrastinator? Procrastination is what keeps you stifled and stagnant. If you were to no longer procrastinate what would you do? Career change? Exercise regimen? Etc.

_____

_____

_____

_____

_____

_____

- What about your personality do you NOT like? What would you change and why?

_____

_____

_____

_____

_____

_____

- Identify things that you liked or did, that your parents did not approve of and tried to change about you.

_____

_____

_____

_____

_____

_____

- What are fears that you experience a difficult time overcoming?

_____

_____

_____

_____

_____

_____

- What are religious and/or cultural beliefs that get in the way of your passion?

_____

_____

_____

_____

_____

_____

- Is your life lacking momentum? In what areas do you feel stuck?

_____

_____

_____

_____

_____

_____

PLAN OF ACTION

1. **Movement.** If stuck in a rut and your passion fails to flow, get moving. Movement can get your brain's endorphins activated, which is a feel-good chemical. Movement of any kind matters. Walking can stimulate thought processes and be a source of relaxation; also dancing, cycling, and yoga. Consequently, when there is little movement, the sedentary life can zap you of vitality and creativity.

2. **Mental Health Day.** Who does not need this from time-to-time? If you are feeling overwhelmed and need a break; for the sake of your mental and emotional health, do so. Of course, the approach to this action plan is specific to your unique life. *YOU* are the only person who is responsible to determine what *YOU* need. If a mental health break is what you need, give it to yourself. Some people find a

way to fit this break into their lives on their day off work, others have to take time off work if the need is severe enough.

3. **Merriment.** Make time for laughter. Having laughter as a regular part of your life can help with passion and possibly minimize frequency of disruption. Merriment can energize you when you are bogged down with the heavy weight life can create; when you are drained and cannot gain footing in your quest to live passionately.

4. **Moments.** Locate moments that stand out for you and highlight them. Keep a journal of these moments, especially if they are monumental. You might be surprised to discover how moments matter as related to your passionate life. Make and keep meaningful moments in your journal and continue to build upon those moments through connections with like-minded people who feed those moments.

5. **Middle-Ground.** This concept refers to balance. Finding your middle-ground of balance is a skill you will do well to hone. When your life is harmonized or balanced, you can more effectively engage in harmonious passions. If you find you are challenged in this area, you will need to discipline yourself over and over, until you improve.

6. **Master.** Finding mastery in a few things is better than having your hands in many things, but experiencing no mastery. When you do not position yourself to master something, you are more likely to experience burnout, and miss out on meaningful life moments. If you find you are neurotically engaging in many things, consider that you might be operating in obsessive passion, and make adjustments.

7. **Massage.** Getting a massage can result in an overall mind and body integrated experience. Massages can prove amazing when you need to relax and enjoy your passion processes. Be sure that you are truly relaxing while receiving a massage. Empty your mind of all thoughts of responsibility and worry, and melt into the experience. In doing so, you can receive the full benefits of massage therapy.

8. **Measure.** Be realistic when you are measuring. Don't put pressure on yourself when setting realistic goals in relation to your passion. Measure how you will accomplish your goals and enjoy the journey. Refrain from comparing and measuring yourself based on what others are doing.

9. **Manage.** Time is what is important here. If you can implement effective time management you can

effectively manage details around your passions. In fact; when you lack effective time-management skills, this could prove as an impediment to your passion. There are many self-help books and literature available to help you in this area.

10. **Memorize.** Keep these concepts in mind. Allow memory of your experiences and all you have learned thus far, to serve as your schoolmaster. Rehearse them so that they become a firm and fixed part of your thought processes. Take a moment to develop concepts and strategies of your own, as specific to your own personality and needs.

CONCLUSION

Passion identifies as a noun, and it expresses like a verb. Passion modifies like an adverb, and it describes as an adjective. This one word serves many functions and speaks to just how pervasive passion is. Passion is so much more than you might have imagined. Passion is a fuel that adds meaning to your life, and keeps your life from being dull and uninspiring.

By now, I am sure you are thinking differently about passion. To what degree depends on how much experience you have with passion. Of everything you have read in this book, of all you have learned before reading this book, and of all you have ever believed about passion; I do not want you to think about passion as a feeling or emotion. Feelings and emotions change frequently. I want you to become grounded in a new ideology or philosophy about passion. Become a passionate thinker. Grind for it and live for it. Guard your passionate mind; you will need it when life experiences and emotions invade and take over. Be intentional so that you will not be left feeling like a hostage to whimsical emotions.

Also, be ever mindful that passion is not only for you. Passion is to be shared with others and exercised pervasively so that your impact is reverberated and felt throughout your realms of influence. In this reading, you have learned that you will face challenges with people and situations. I suggest that you remain aware of relationships specifically. Like nothing else, relationships will test you. If you are not careful; relationships can be kryptonite to your passion. Why do I impress relationships? Because relationships that you care about can be a huge challenge, especially when your passion is connected to people.

Relationships are important, as I stressed in the reading, but relationships need balance and boundaries in order to be considered as healthy connections. If you are not strong in this area, do the work of developing boundaries and balance. In a training recently, I learned something that I will pass on to you. The speaker quoted Eddy, B. (2008): It's All Your Fault! 12 Tips for

Managing People Who Blame Others for Everything. Eddy posits that it is important to be an effective communicator when dealing with difficult people. One way to implement effective communication is to convey information in an effective manner; and also, give an "E.A.R."

In this example, Eddy states that E stands for Empathy, A stands for Attention, and R stands for Respect. Listen attentively, with a heart and mind of respect and empathy. There are no guarantees things will go smoothly. However; you will be proud of yourself for demonstrating effective communication that others can learn from, should they decide to do so.

Don't waste another moment. Time is continuously passing and you have so much to do. You have much to contribute. You are a piece of the puzzle of something larger; and yes, you are essential. You might be older in life and you might be doubting. You might tell yourself that it is too late for you, and others might tell you this as well. Let me tell you, this is a lie. It is never to late to do *something* for which you have passion. You are still breathing, living, and moving; you can discover and express your life of passion.

I introduce to you, Ernestine. She is currently in her eighties. Ernestine can be a source of encouragement for almost anyone. She states she began working out when she was 56 years-old. She then became a personal trainer and a competitive bodybuilder. Her story can be googled to learn more about her tenacity and grit, to do what she can and what she has passion for. This is her story. Now is the time to craft and sculpt your own story. Do whatever you need to do to get it done, but by all means; do it! If going back to school might be helpful, do it. If gearing yourself to gain more certifications in your current career is necessary, do it. If relocating can help you, do it.

You might feel stuck and stifled, and unaware of who you are, what you want, and what you like; but push through all of this and endeavor. The more you explore and the more self-awareness you can experience, the greater your chances of overcoming doubt, challenges, and self-defeating messages. My final encouragement to you is in the form of an exercise. This exercise is commonly used in therapy; it is called flowers and bubbles. Whenever you feel overwhelmed; you need to relax, of course. Relaxing can help you to become centered and refocused. Then you can continue on in your pursuit of passion. In this activity you will need to have a seat in a relaxing atmosphere. With your eyes closed, breath in gently as if you are smelling flowers, then slowly blow out as if you are blowing bubbles to relax your diaphragm. That's it, you got it! Now repeat as often as you need, smelling flowers and blowing bubbles. Enjoy your life of unleashed, unstoppable passion. Once you start, who can stop it?

GRATITUDES

A HUMBLE APPRECIATION AND A WARM THANK YOU—

To Candace Smith, you are a huge part of the reason I am writing this book. Your fervor, knowledge, and spiritual excitement are refreshing. I also appreciate your willingness, without hesitation, to write the foreword for this book.

To my husband, for your ability to know when I needed to take a break to rest my fingers and eyes, for turning the television to comedy and getting me out of the serious zone at times, for your quirky sense of humor that made things a little lighthearted, and for reading through and listening to me read entries as I developed this manuscript.

To my daughter, Dawn; you inspire me in ways you might not realize. Your strength reminds me of some of the reasons I am passionate about life. You make me laugh out loud and make living intentionally a joy.

To my son, Joshua; your wisdom and sharing conversations with me about growth and development have been significant in directing some of my thoughts as I developed this material. As I write, I hear some of our conversations. Also, your youthful, comical way about life keeps me inspired and energized.

To my mother and Paul, who support me with their physical presence, energy, and encouraging words; these serve as reminders to keep at it.

To my siblings who are a source of encouragement.

To my dear friend, Justin Smart; your ears are always available and your heart is always open. Thank you for allowing me to vent and process information with you, and thank you for your prayers.

Last but certainly not least, I thank God for the passion and knowledge to learn and impart information unselfishly. My goals and desires are to always have a mindset to pay it forward!

Recommended for You

Chodron, P. (1997). When Things Fall Apart: heart advice for difficult times. Shambhala Publications. Boston, MA.

Crabb, L. (1988). Inside Out. NavPress Publishing Group. Colorado Springs, CO.

Crabb, L. (1997). Connecting: healing for ourselves and our relationships. World Publishing. Nashville, TN.

Crabb, L. (1999). The Safest Place on Earth: where people connect and are forever changed. World Publishing. Nashville, TN.

Gordon, J. (2007). The Energy Bus. John Wiley and Sons, Inc. Hoboken, New Jersey.

Gordon, J. (2012). The Positive Dog. John Wiley and Sons, Inc. Hoboken, New Jersey.

Johnson, S. (2002). Who Moved My Cheese? G.P. Putman Sons. New York, NY.

Morrissey, M. (1996). Building Your Field of Dreams. Bantam Books. Broadway, New York.

Ruiz, D.M. (1997). The Four Agreements. Amber-Allen Publishing. San Rafael, CA.

Scott-Lindsey, C. (2018). Communication and You: explore issues and enhance relationships. Christian Faith Publishing. Meadville, PA.

Scott-Lindsey, C. (2018). How Can I Laugh When Nothing's Funny: understanding and overcoming depression. Authorhouse. Bloomington, IN.

About the Author

Crystal Scott is a Licensed Marriage and Family Therapist in the states of California, Texas, and Michigan. She holds a Master's Degree in Counseling Psychology as well as a certificate in Pastoral Counseling from Holy Names University, Oakland, CA. Crystal graduated Magna cum Laude with a Bachelor's of Science Degree in Organizational Management from Patten University, Oakland CA. Her primary private practice location is in the DFW Texas Region, which she established over 7 years ago after relocating from the California, San Francisco Bay Area. Crystal opened her second private practice location in Detroit Michigan 4 years ago. She has been in her role as therapist for approximately 17 years. Her credentials afford her opportunities to provide critical incident and stress debriefing (CISD) services to many organizations and employment companies. Crystal also facilitates teaching and training on various topics for mental health, coping, and employee assistance needs. Additionally, Crystal is the author of *Take Back Your Life, Sin and the Church, Communication and You, and How Can I Laugh?*

NOTES

NOTES

NOTES

NOTES

NOTES

NOTES

NOTES

NOTES

NOTES

NOTES

Printed in the United States
By Bookmasters